Keeping the Chattahoochee

Keeping the Chattahoochee

REVIVING AND DEFENDING A GREAT SOUTHERN RIVER

Sally Sierer Bethea

The University of Georgia Press
Athens

A Wormsloe
FOUNDATION
nature book

© 2023 by the University of Georgia Press
Athens, Georgia 30602
www.ugapress.org
All rights reserved
Designed by Mary McKeon
Set in Adobe Caslon Pro by Mary McKeon
Printed and bound by Sheridan

The paper in this book meets the guidelines for
permanence and durability of the Committee on
Production Guidelines for Book Longevity of the
Council on Library Resources.

Most University of Georgia Press titles are
available from popular e-book vendors.

Printed in the United States of America

23 24 25 26 27 C 5 4 3 2

Library of Congress Cataloging-in-Publication Data
Names: Bethea, Sally Sierer, 1951– author.
Title: Keeping the Chattahoochee : reviving and defending a great Southern river /
Sally Sierer Bethea.
Description: Athens : The University of Georgia Press, [2023] | Series: Wormsloe
Foundation nature books | Includes bibliographical references.
Identifiers: LCCN 2022062215 | ISBN 9780820364322 (hardback) | ISBN 9780820364339 (epub) |
ISBN 9780820364346 (pdf)
Subjects: LCSH: Environmentalism—United States. | Environmental policy—United States.
| Chattahoochee River—Environmental conditions. | Chattahoochee River Valley—
Environmental conditions. | Bethea, Sally Sierer, 1951—Travel—Chattahoochee River. |
Riverkeepers—United States. | Environmentalists—United States. |
Ecologists—United States.
Classification: LCC GE197 .b478 2023 | DDC 333.91/62160975—dc23/eng20230422
LC record available at https://lccn.loc.gov/2022062215

*To Charles and Robert—my adventurous, literary, and loving sons,
whose sense of wonder in nature inspires me.*

AND

*To Neill—my knowledgeable partner, advocate, and walking companion,
who supported every aspect of this book from its conception.*

I've known rivers:
I've known rivers ancient as the world and
older than the flow of blood in human veins.

My soul has grown deep like the rivers.

I bathed in the Euphrates when dawns were young.
I built my hut near the Congo and it lulled me to sleep.
I looked upon the Nile and raised the pyramids above it.
I heard the singing of the Mississippi when Abe Lincoln
went down to New Orleans, and I've seen its muddy bosom
turn all golden in the sunset.

I've known rivers:
Ancient, dusky rivers.

My soul has grown deep like the rivers.

—*Langston Hughes, "The Negro Speaks of Rivers" (1925)*

CONTENTS

PREFACE

Tell me, what is it you plan to do with your one wild and precious life?
—Mary Oliver

I grew up beside two small streams that converged behind my home on the outskirts of Atlanta, Georgia, in the 1950s and 1960s. These clear waterways, which flowed through the large, wooded lots in our mid-twentieth century neighborhood, were full of minnows, crayfish, and snakes. As a young girl, I wondered where the water went when it left our yard.

One summer, I recruited my sister and a friend to follow our unnamed stream through woods and neighbors' backyards, exploring the meandering watercourse with its gold-flecked rocks and rippling currents. Years later, I learned that my childhood stream (or creek) flows into Nancy Creek, then Peachtree Creek, and finally the Chattahoochee River.

Like many children, I loved playing in the creek and falling asleep to the soothing sound of flowing water outside my bedroom window and the hooting owls in the trees: my pocket of nature. I was a city girl with a love of the natural world and a predilection for adventure, both of which have stayed with me all my life.

On what was then a largely undeveloped island off the west coast of Florida, my family found a special place where we vacationed as I grew up. We collected shells on its beaches, visited the wildlife refuge that comprises a third of Sanibel Island, boated and fished with friends, and painted watercolors of coconut palms waving in the ocean breezes. We watched the ever-changing shoreline, altered through the seasons and years by wind, waves, and currents.

We hunted fossil shells on the banks of the Caloosahatchee River, sifting through the sandy marl to find specimens that were millions of years old, yet still had shiny patinas. In the backwaters of mangrove swamps, we waded barefoot—at times in waist-deep water—cautiously exploring the muddy bottom with our toes, seeking king's crown conches.

A large, climbable driftwood tree, polished by sand and wind, became an imaginary house with ocean views from every room, and a special driftwood "key" allowed entrance. My parents loved Sanibel's wild nature—its red mangrove forests, flocks of roseate spoonbills, and rare junonia shells—and did what they could to help preserve it. At a young age, I learned the importance of advocating for the things you love, especially those that are voiceless.

When planes flew low over the island's beaches during the postwar 1950s and early 1960s—spraying clouds of the insecticide DDT to kill mosquitoes—we ran outside, excited to see the old war bombers. We waved at the pilots, who were visible through the plane windows. The poisonous legacy of DDT and other chemical "wonders" was years from being revealed to the public by a courageous scientist and brilliant writer named Rachel Carson.

Carson's book *Silent Spring*, published in 1962, ignited fierce opposition from the chemical and agricultural industries and helped inspire today's environmental movement. A decade later, after being designated a probable human carcinogen, DDT was finally banned in the United States; however, it continues to contaminate ecosystems and can still be found in animal tissue.

My mother survived three different cancers, including lymphoma, during her ninety-four years. In my mind's eye, I can still see, and wonder about, the effect of those planes and the white clouds of poison that they regularly spread across our island—just as other aircraft spread DDT across croplands, forests, and gardens throughout America.

During my college years, beginning in the late 1960s, I studied social justice issues: civil rights, poverty, and mental health. I also found time to camp and hike in the Southern Appalachians with friends, strengthening both body and mind. Walking in nature and listening to its music has never failed to lift and renew my spirits, helping me find the truth in the common language of all living things. After college, and back home, I looked for opportunities to meet people, further explore Georgia's natural beauty, and find ways to advocate for a healthy environment for all.

In the mid-1970s, I attended my first meeting of the local chapter of the Sierra Club, the national organization established in 1892 by wilderness advocate and environmental philosopher John Muir. I recall my immediate affinity for the people I met there; they were friendly and passionate about fighting for rivers, forests, and coastline. The club's outings program offered easy access to wilderness areas, mountain ridges, barrier islands, and new acquaintances. I became a volunteer and club officer. I had found the circle of people who would become my friends and colleagues. One of the original "river rats" who helped lead what began as a ragtag movement to save the Chattahoochee River became my mentor and lifelong friend.

Realizing that I needed to be better informed to become an effective advocate, I entered graduate school at Georgia Tech in 1978, supported by a scholarship for minorities; in those days, as a woman, I qualified. Two years later, with a master's degree in environmental planning, I found a way to channel my budding conservation ethic into a career and honed my advocacy skills by working for the government and nonprofits.

When my two sons were in middle and elementary school and I was in my early forties, I had the chance to become the first riverkeeper for the Upper Chattahoochee, a job that required creating a new nonprofit organization devoted to restoring and defending the hardworking waterway.

Cutting through the heart of the Deep South, the Chattahoochee sustains nearly five million people with water to drink, opportunities to fish and swim, and places to renew their spirits. An essential part of that work is safeguarding the tributaries that flow into the Chattahoochee, including those streams behind my childhood home. For two decades, I worked with an eclectic range of people to restore our river—a demanding but gratifying task. We made real progress together, for which I am very grateful. I retired in 2014 and handed the reins of the organization to two trusted individuals who I had hired and worked side-by-side with for years.

Retirement has been a time of reflection, a chance to finally slow down and more closely examine the world around me, especially the beauty and detail that I often rushed past while I was mothering and riverkeeping. I hoped to find intimacy in a local landscape where nature would be my teacher. I wanted to learn how to be more attentive, how to focus on the smaller things that we notice—but do not really see—every day of our lives.

For more than a year, I regularly walked a path to the Chattahoochee that travels along a creek and through a forest with old-growth remnants. I learned how to be more attentive: how to "adopt the pace of nature," as Ralph Waldo Emerson counseled.

These walks through the seasons summoned memories and stories—from joyous and funny to frustrating and even alarming—about the people, adventures, challenges, and celebrations that filled my two decades of working to restore the Chattahoochee. Together, we helped give the river a voice.

I wrote this book with two purposes in mind. First, to inspire you to find your own special place in nature. To magnify your sense of wonder and awe, by focusing on those smaller things we rarely take note of. To learn how all of us—all living species—are truly and essentially connected. To quote poet Mary Oliver, we are a "family of things."

My hope is that my walks and observations, recounted at the beginning of each chapter, will draw you into the Chattahoochee watershed and open your eyes and heart to the wondrous variety of plants, animals, and people that inhabit our planet. The experience can be life changing.

My second purpose is to offer guidance and hope to those of you motivated to safeguard our natural resources, whether they be rivers, coastlines, wilderness, wildlife, or your neighborhood park. This means, of course, that you are working for the health and survival of all of us—our family.

Each of my walks to the river prompted memories from my two decades as the riverkeeper for the Chattahoochee. These remembrances are captured here in stories that illustrate our effort to revive our neglected river. They include the strategies and challenges, the lessons learned, and the strengths we gained along the way, much of which could be summarized in one word: persistence.

My journey to become the best possible environmental advocate—and to better understand myself—is woven through these stories. Like memories, these tales are not sequential in their telling. They move forward and backward in time. In this way, memories are unlike rivers.

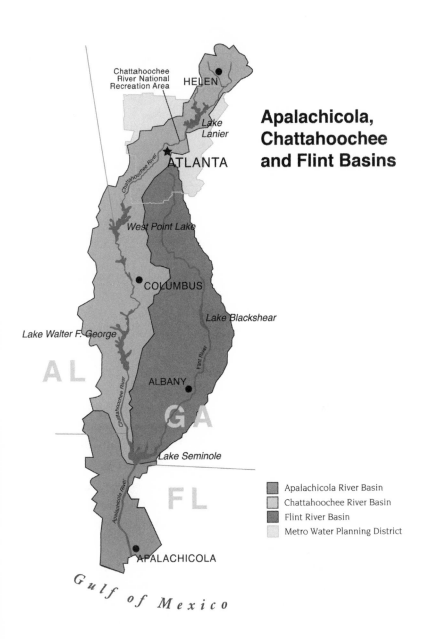

Illustration of the Apalachicola-Chattahoochee-Flint River Basin, which drains approximately twenty thousand square miles of land in Georgia, Alabama, and Florida.
Credit: Chattahoochee Riverkeeper.

Keeping the Chattahoochee

The ruins of a cabin built in the 1930s or 1940s sit near the banks of the Chattahoochee River, overlooking Devils Race Course Shoals. Photo: Henry Jacobs.

CHAPTER 1

Keeping Secretary Babbitt Dry

May 8, 2019

The sun shines not on us, but in us.
The rivers flow not past us, but through us.
—*John Muir*

On a beautiful, windy day in early May, I set forth in search of a locally beloved bamboo forest, a short distance from my home in midtown Atlanta. Nearing the forest, I drive along a paved road lined with expensive homes, what was once a Native American trail. Where the pavement ends, a narrow dirt road continues to follow the ridge, leading me into the forested landscape of the East Palisades unit of the Chattahoochee River National Recreation Area.

After parking my car in a designated area, I walk back down the access road, study a posted map, and turn onto a worn path. It leads downhill toward the river—passing, crossing, and sometimes winding above wooded ravines, rocky outcrops, and small streams that converge to become Cabin Creek, a tributary of the Chattahoochee River, whose waters I worked to protect for more than two decades.

The clear water in the streams is noisy, gurgling as it falls over rocks, summoning memories of the streams behind my childhood home. The hardwood forest in the creek's ravine is filled with oaks, tulip poplars, sourwoods, magnolias, and beeches. A few spring wildflowers are still blooming in the woods, but most are long gone. I look forward to seeing the beauties that will undoubtedly emerge from the loamy, rich soil next spring before the dense tree canopy diminishes the sunlight reaching the ground.

The stone ruins of an old cabin lie where the creek trail ends at the Chattahoochee's shoreline and intersects a second trail that winds along the river. The structure is believed to have been built in the 1930s or 1940s for hunting, drinking whiskey, and playing cards, according to a longtime park ranger. There's also a small stone bridge over the creek and a spring house upslope, but it will be weeks before I notice the bridge under the thick vegetation and months before I find the spring house in the woods.

The river is high, hurrying downstream through Devils Race Course Shoals, then curving dramatically to the right past several islands, one called Charlie's Island for the founder of a local canoeing group. According to park ranger Jerry Hightower, there is some evidence that a bridge once crossed from the shoreline near the cabin to the island.

It hasn't rained recently, so the high river must be the result of a torrent of water being released from Lake Lanier through Buford Dam, more than forty miles upstream. The dam was constructed by the federal government in the 1950s to generate power, control floods, and provide enough water to float barges far downstream. Today, attempts to make use of the water behind the dam for other downstream needs, such as water supply, irrigation, and ecosystem health, have sparked endless conflict.

I can't see Diving Rock—a chunk of granite about twenty-five feet above the river from which local daredevils like to jump into the deep water—but I know it's there, just a few hundred yards beyond the islands, across from the beach at Sandy Point. Seeing the Chattahoochee from this shoreline perspective for the very first time, rather than from my kayak in the river, I am astonished. I have stumbled on a place where water, rocks, sky, and trees create a majestic panorama. It's a startling new perspective on a scene I thought I already knew well.

As I walk upstream along the river, mountain laurel shrubs (*Kalmia latifolia*) are blooming, flanked by doghobble bushes (*Leucothoe fontanesiana*); laurel petals carpet the ground beneath them. I cross a stream on a dilapidated wooden bridge and pass beside tall rock outcrops that form an impenetrable slope, requiring the trail to negotiate a narrow stretch of land between the craggy palisades and the river.

The bamboo forest, with its three-story, bright green stalks, materializes before me. This nonnative member of the grass family is one of the fastest-growing plants on earth—able to quickly choke out natural vegetation. Although I am concerned about its impact on the park, I am still mesmerized by the tall silhouettes along the riverbank: dark stalks backlit by the sunlight flooding the Chattahoochee.

Two hours in the woods and at the river have passed like minutes. It's time to head home. I have made a decision. I have found a special place, a corner of nature that I will explore through the seasons.

Switching between the past, present, and future, I think about the yearlong adventure of walks that lie ahead. A memory of an incident that occurred just upstream of Diving Rock emerges from my early years as riverkeeper.

In 1994 I began my duties as the first full-time riverkeeper for the upper half of the Chattahoochee River—from its damp beginnings at a spring in the north Georgia mountains to West Point Lake, a man-made reservoir (or lake) located midway down the most heavily used waterway in Georgia.

Four hundred thirty-five miles downstream of this spring, the Chattahoochee converges with the Flint River at the Georgia-Florida border and becomes the Apalachicola River. The Flint rises under the concrete runways of Hartsfield-Jackson Atlanta International Airport and flows nearly 350 miles through rural farmland and forests to its meeting with the Chattahoochee. The mingled waters that drain from land in Georgia, Alabama, and Florida flow into Apalachicola Bay—one of the most biologically productive estuaries in the country—and then into the Gulf of Mexico.

Working out of donated space in the basement of an office building near the river, Upper Chattahoochee Riverkeeper set about to keep watch over the river for people and wildlife. Nearly two decades after it was established, the organization expanded its mission to include the entire length of the Chattahoochee and its tributaries downstream to the Florida border, becoming Chattahoochee Riverkeeper (Riverkeeper).

With cofounders Laura Turner Seydel and Rutherford Seydel, along with approval from the international Waterkeeper Alliance and a confidence-boosting seed grant from the Turner Foundation, Riverkeeper embarked on a journey to save the Chattahoochee. Plagued by chronic sewage spills, uncontrolled urban growth, dirty storm runoff, industrial toxins, trash, and overuse, the river was repeatedly named one of the most endangered rivers in the country.

In addition to curbing pollution, Riverkeeper's work includes defending the environmental laws, policies, and budgets passed to safeguard waterways like the Chattahoochee—as well as protected places along its banks. The Chattahoochee River National Recreation Area (CRNRA) is one such protected place. This unit of the national park system, established in 1978 by then-president Jimmy Carter, includes a forty-eight-mile section of the Chattahoochee that flows through metro Atlanta's northern suburbs to the western edge of the city.

⮾⮾⮾

In 1995 U.S. secretary of the interior Bruce Babbitt visited the CRNRA. At the time, he was on a tour around the country to rally attention to an attempt by some federal legislators to close urban units of the national park system, including our river park; the supposed rationale was to cut costs. When the proposal was finally dropped months later, Babbitt, an ardent supporter of national parks, said, "The House [of Representatives] appears to have finally heard the American people."

The superintendent of the CRNRA invited me to join the group that would accompany Babbitt on a short canoe trip from Powers Island to Sandy Point, the beach across from Diving Rock. As media and onlookers assembled at the Powers Island put-in, the superintendent motioned to me. "Why don't you paddle with the secretary?" he said.

I was not, and am not, an expert canoeist, much preferring a single kayak. I hesitated for a split second. I imaged flipping Bruce Babbitt in the river, with footage all over the evening news. Not for the last time in my riverkeeping career, I decided to push myself into uncharted waters.

Babbitt, who outweighed me by some seventy-five pounds, was helped into the bow. I took the stern. We floated downstream with the secretary holding his paddle in his lap. Eventually, we entered the fast-moving water of Devils Race Course Shoals, approaching the hard-right turn past the islands on our way to Sandy Point.

Another canoe paddled toward ours. Inside it was a reporter with WSB-TV, a local television station known for its environmental reporting, along with his cameraman and the head of another nonprofit. They were all large men. Reaching toward us with an extended boom mic, the reporter attempted to carry on a conversation with the secretary, but he leaned too far out of his boat. Suddenly, his canoe flipped, in full view of the media and guests waiting on the beach at Sandy Point.

Cameras onshore were rolling as I managed to steer our canoe past the midriver mess, around the islands, and to shore with Babbitt strangely silent in the bow. Were such events all in a day's work for the secretary, I wondered. The occupants of the other canoe were fine—just wet and embarrassed.

I remember breathing a huge sigh of relief, not knowing then how many times over the next twenty years I would do other things far outside my comfort zone on behalf of the river. Some would end well, like this paddle trip, at least for the secretary and me. Others would best be described as character building. That night, several rival TV stations gave ample time to the canoe-flipping episode.

CHAPTER 2
Restoring a Farmer's Stream

May 15, 2019

A week later, as spring moves toward summer, the forest feels thicker and looks greener. My attention is drawn to the magnificent trees that grow in the rich soil on the north-facing slopes of the Cabin Creek ravine: huge tulip poplars, beeches, oaks, magnolias, sweetgums, pines, and more. The face that a slope presents to the sun plays a major role in its microclimate and the types of plants that colonize there. North-facing slopes, for example, are cooler and moister with a greater diversity of plant species.

It is doubtful that any farming or building has occurred in these woods in the past one hundred–plus years, according to local naturalist Kathryn Kolb. The steep slopes, narrow stream corridors, and protected remnants of the original forest are signs that the area was not easily accessible to humans. The soil and plant life have remained relatively untouched: no plowing, digging, scraping, compacting, or amending for at least four generations. Essential minerals and nutrients from decomposing animal and plant matter have enriched this soil, which is providing ecosystem services, like water filtration.

I anticipate the river this time and hear it before my eyes can confirm that it is flowing fast and full. Again, it takes my breath away: as the trail turns, the understory opens, and I can see the silver-green water. The air at the river smells of freshly cut watermelon. A favorite wildflower, spiderwort (*Tradescantia*), is blooming in several places. Gorgeous pale pink flowers of the Carolina rhododendron (*Rhododendron minus*) contrast with the shrub's dark green foliage.

As I walk upriver on the trail, I find two trees leaning on, and wrapping around, each other in an arboreal embrace. A river birch and a maple are entwined in what must be a decades-long reliance on each other. They appear to be healthy trees that have found stability by settling into each other for balance and support—an angle of repose.

It is a busy day on the trail. A couple carries a deflated raft and pump from a downstream parking area. They tell me they're hiking to the upper end of the river trail, where they plan to inflate the small raft and float back down to their car. Two young men carry climbing gear to scale the rock outcrops. There are trail runners and I can see more rafts on the far side of the river.

I pick up as much shoreline trash as I can carry in my arms and pockets, making a mental note to bring bags next time. Small pieces of Styrofoam dominate, along with plastic wrappers, a few plastic bottles, and other detritus; their origins were likely upstream lawns, roads, and parking lots.

In the dappled light of the forest, I watch the river flow past and then head back uphill, thinking about the thin, fragile layer of organic and inorganic material upon which all life depends: soil. A small word for such a tremendous gift.

Several years ago, I joined Kathryn Kolb to learn about soils and remnant old-growth forests in Atlanta. We explored the hardwoods on a steep slope in the West Palisades unit of the Chattahoochee River National Recreation Area, across the river from Cabin Creek. Kathryn explained that Atlanta is unique among major cities in the country for the number of large, wooded areas with old trees and undisturbed soils that build biologically diverse habitats.

After the Civil War, much of the metro region stayed in a depressed and rural condition for many decades. Atlanta's expansion did not begin in earnest until the 1960s. This delay allowed pockets of the original forests in our area to survive, including those in the national park, whose lands were protected with federal ownership beginning a decade later.

Soil is full of life. This upper layer of earth provides habitat for billions of microorganisms that absorb dissolved organic material, recycling matter and nutrients through the process of decomposition. The organisms that promote the growth and life cycles of native species include fungi, bacteria, protozoa, microarthropods, and nematodes, collectively known as a soil microbiome. Stability comes from such diversity; however, these organisms can be easily disturbed, and often destroyed, by human activities. Highly beneficial, soil microbiomes can prevent soil erosion and loss of nutrients, help plants fight pathogens and toxins, and sustain soil fertility for food production. They also act as a carbon sink (absorbing more carbon from the atmosphere than is released) and help preserve biodiversity.

When people ask me to name the top threats to the Chattahoochee and its watershed—the area of land where precipitation collects and drains off into the river—I always mention soil erosion. When rain falls on land that is partially or completely denuded of vegetation, soil particles will dislodge and flow rapidly downhill in cascades of muddy water. Construction sites in urbanizing areas and dirt roads and agricultural and forestry activities in rural areas are the usual sources of this pollution when steps are not taken to keep soil on site.

Erosion control practices include minimizing and phasing land disturbances, planting vegetated buffers, and installing fiber mats, silt fences, and rock check dams. When the soil particles begin to move downslope, they can pick up oils, industrial waste, chemicals, pesticides, bacteria, and other substances and carry them piggyback to the nearest waterway. Once sediment enters a river or lake, the cost to treat drinking water may increase and favorite fishing holes may be destroyed. Property values of downstream river or lakefront landowners can also be reduced by the unattractive appearance of dirty water.

The trees, shrubs, and plants that grow naturally next to a river, creek, or lake—called riparian (streamside) buffers—filter the contaminants from storm runoff and stabilize riverbanks. When these buffers are damaged or removed, the erosion problems worsen exponentially and it becomes difficult, if not impossible, to stop erosion and the loss of land, including communities of microorganisms.

On a small farm in north Georgia, Riverkeeper learned that the prevention of soil erosion is much more cost effective than trying to fix these problems after the fact.

Sweeping his hand across his land, Justin Savage said, "I'll tell you what. This stream is eating away my pasture." A cattle and chicken farmer, Savage had owned property on the Left Fork of the Soque River in north Georgia for many years. By the late 1990s, he was losing as much as one hundred tons of rich mountain soil per year into the severely eroding trout stream.

Savage's property was disappearing—half an acre in just a few years, he claimed—into the watercourse, which flows nearly thirty miles through hilly terrain before entering the Chattahoochee. On one tight stream meander on his land, six-foot vertical banks were regularly sloughing into the water. The erosion was the result of dredging, channeling, clearing, grading, and riprapping (rock armoring) along upstream waterways. Making matters worse, Savage's livestock regularly trampled vegetation attempting to grow at the water's edge.

Jennifer Derby, a knowledgeable and intrepid scientist with the U.S. Environmental Protection Agency (EPA), worked closely with Riverkeeper to secure funding and technical support to develop a plan to restore the trout stream. The water channel needed to be reconfigured to a more natural shape, the banks replanted, and the cattle fenced away from the water. The goal: to bring the stream back into balance in terms of the water it must usually carry and the amount and type of materials—sand, rocks, and pebbles—that it must transport.

After a year of planning, a 1,300-foot section of the stream was reshaped to restore natural curves and resize the channel, allowing it to carry water and sediment with minimal erosion. Large rocks and trees with their root wads (root masses) were strategically placed in the stream to deflect flow away from vulnerable banks and enhance habitat. We secured all necessary environmental permits for the massive project. Equipment and materials included four hundred tons of rocks, sixteen trees, several pieces of heavy machinery, and erosion control products to stabilize the banks.

Hundreds of hours of labor were provided by Riverkeeper staff, federal scientists, state biologists, students, local businesses, and volunteers—some of whom camped at the site to be ready for the long workdays. The project was expensive, even with materials and equipment provided at reduced costs and the assistance of EPA scientists.

When it was completed in 1998, the stream restoration became the first project in Georgia to repair a degraded waterway using pioneering techniques based on fluvial geomorphology: an understanding of the way water flow affects the shape of a stream channel and surrounding landforms. The project was called a showcase for the emerging science of natural stream restoration. Upon completion, soil erosion was at near-undetectable levels in the newly stabilized environment. Savage was thrilled, and so were we.

"Return of a river," proclaimed the *Atlanta Journal-Constitution*—next to a color photo of Riverkeeper staffer Katherine Baer standing triumphantly beside the restored trout stream. The positive news story about the Chattahoochee was much celebrated, given the constant but necessary coverage of the daily pollution crises downstream in Georgia's capital city.

On a spring evening, I drove north from the city for an event hosted by the Soque River Watershed Association at the restoration site. It was the first time I'd visited the area in more than a decade. As I got out of the car and walked toward the stream, I almost wept. Tall, healthy trees lined the banks with native species growing beneath them in the stable, loamy soil. The cold mountain stream, in which I could see several trout in the shadows, meandered slowly and naturally on its way down to the Chattahoochee.

CHAPTER 3
Loving a River, Telling Her Story

May 22, 2019

Whoever you are, no matter how lonely, the world offers itself to your imagination, … over and over announcing your place in the family of things.
—*Mary Oliver*

On my third visit to Cabin Creek, I am relatively relaxed—not so anxious to see everything at once. I am beginning to unlearn hurrying. More familiar with the rugged trail, I focus on the details of trees, plants, roots, water, and rocks.

A tangle of roots—really an artful, natural weaving—grows over bare rock between the earth and the creek. The roots extend the length of a walking stick from soil to water, where their tips bend down into the stream. Some are firmly planted in its bed: living straws for the nearby tulip poplar tree they sustain. The exposed tops of the roots have been worn smooth by hikers. I wonder how many of these visitors to the woods have noticed the roots and their heroic effort to reach the liquid that ensures their tree's survival.

I meet half a dozen people and several dogs on the trail today. Wildlife seems more abundant. For the first time, I notice gnats and bees buzzing in the woods, along with more active squirrels and chipmunks. From a rosette of leaves on the ground beside the trail, square-stemmed stalks rise about a foot above the base. They are covered with buds that I know will soon bloom in pale blue to violet colors. It's lyreleaf sage (*Salvia lyrata*), a wild-growing perennial herb.

Near the confluence of Cabin Creek and the river, I discover a patch of dwarf, or small-flowered, pawpaw shrubs (*Asimina parviflora*); the leaves of this shrub are the only plants that the zebra swallowtail butterfly (*Eurytides marcellus*) caterpillars will eat. The deciduous pawpaw tree (*Asimina triloba*), a relative of the dwarf pawpaw, produces the largest edible fruit of any native tree in the country. It is often called "America's forgotten fruit." Individuals can weigh up to a pound and grow to six inches in length; the rich flesh is enjoyed by a variety of animals, including humans.

The river is high again, covering the rocky shoals, but it seems to be dropping, based on

A red-eared slider or red-eared terrapin (*Trachemys scripta elegans*) suns on a log in the Chattahoochee River. Photo: Tom Wilson.

wet riverbanks that indicate the Chattahoochee was several feet higher earlier in the day. Swallowtail butterflies (tiger, *Papilio glaucus*, and black, *Papilio polyxenes*) fly past me on the trail, lighting on nearby bushes; their ancestors are believed to have developed an impressive two hundred million years ago, before flowering plants emerged.

A turtle eases into the water from a log near the shore. On the river, pairs of mallard ducks (*Anas platyrhynchos*) mingle with the geese (*Branta canadensis*). One goose takes advantage of the river's wave train, effortlessly bobbing up and down, as she floats through the shoals.

At the end of the river trail, I find a large rock, slightly hidden behind shrubs and comfortable for sitting. A few feet from my perch, more mallards and geese parade upstream along the shore, single file, with the geese leading the way. The wind feels good on my face as I sit and watch the river rush headlong toward the distant sea. I'm finding my own place in the Chattahoochee's diverse family of living things.

As I walk back uphill to my car, carrying a bag of trash, I spot white blooms out of the corner of my eye, about fifteen feet off the trail on a north-facing slope. A closer look reveals that what appeared at a distance to be single, pod-shaped blooms are clusters of tiny flowers not unlike hyacinths.

I've found fly poison (*Amianthium muscitoxicum*)—a plant that is not overly common in metro Atlanta; all parts of it are poisonous, with the bulbs being the most toxic. Early settlers ground the bulbs into a paste and mixed it with sugar or honey to attract and kill flies. Cherokees used it topically to stop itching. Since precolonial times, medicinal plants—usually found in stable, biodiverse habitats—have been used for healing.

Biodiversity is a measure of the variety and variability of all life forms—plants, animals, and microorganisms—and the ecosystems they inhabit. A river ecosystem includes the flowing waters that drain a landscape (watershed) and the interactions among living and nonliving things (rocks, weather, climate) from the river's source (headwaters) to its mouth at a bay, sea, or ocean. From Riverkeeper's earliest days, we sought ways to tell the Chattahoochee's story of biodiversity and beauty in words and images.

Like other rivers around the world, the Chattahoochee provides, at no cost, a liquid lifeline that for thousands of years has connected and nourished a large, diverse family of things: communities of people, wildlife, and plants.

Until the mid-twentieth century—when a scientist at the University of

Georgia pioneered the concept of ecosystems—few understood the environment as a system of interdependent biological communities, including humans. With his groundbreaking research, Eugene Odum revealed that the environment is "a complex, biological economy of shared resources, competition, and cooperation." As he often said, "The ecosystem is greater than the sum of its parts." In graduate school at Georgia Tech in the late 1970s, I devoured his landmark book, *The Fundamentals of Ecology*, written for a wide audience and first published in 1953.

To understand how a river ecosystem works, a basic grasp of river basin geography is indispensable. It can foster an appreciation of one's place in the larger, watery landscape and spark curiosity and questions. Are you located in the headwaters, where the Chattahoochee is tiny, or in southwest Georgia, where the river is wide but slowed by large dams? Where is your drinking water sourced? Where does your dirty household wastewater go once it's been treated? Where is the water going in the streams that you cross in your daily commute, and where did that water come from? What animals and birds depend on the waterways near you?

Learning how rivers work and how they connect and sustain living communities is empowering. Climate change, population growth, and burgeoning water conflicts demand that we become more river and water intelligent.

A local writer and publisher named Fred Brown contacted Riverkeeper a few years after the organization was established. He suggested that Riverkeeper work collaboratively with him and Sherri M. L. Smith to produce the first-ever comprehensive guide to the Chattahoochee. It would trace the river from north Georgia to Florida's Apalachicola Bay. We enthusiastically accepted the offer. The project's potential was clear. The guide could help people not only navigate the waters of the Chattahoochee and its riverside trails but also begin to think about the bigger picture: the entire river system and the interdependence among its diverse communities. Compelling stories about people, history, and ecology would illustrate these relationships. *The Riverkeeper's Guide to the Chattahoochee* was published in 1997 and celebrated at events throughout the watershed.

Recently, I looked at the cover of the guidebook, a gorgeous photograph of a simple rowboat on the water in evening light. With some image manipulation, it looks like a painting. No one is in the boat, but the oars are positioned for immediate use and the message is obvious. Hop in and head downstream. Explore the river. Learn about her history and the many ways she sustains millions of people, plants, and wildlife. Admire her beauty and lament her pollution. Live a fluvial life.

The book provides the how-to, where-to information on boating, fishing, and hiking and describes what you'll see along the way. Profiles of river experts, biologists, fishing guides, naturalists, historians—and regular folks who love the Chattahoochee—provide local color and interesting context. The pen-and-ink illustrations are wonderful.

Until I recently turned the book over and looked at the back cover, I had forgotten that actress Jane Fonda and politician Newt Gingrich provided testimonials—another example of the way a river welcomes diversity, bringing together not only allies but also political adversaries.

I remember the evening of the photo shoot that resulted in the cover image. A few years earlier, I had met and helped Joe Cook and Monica Sheppard, both writers and photographers, on their one-hundred-day canoe expedition down the Chattahoochee, from the mountains to the sea, in 1995. (In 2000 Joe and Monica published *River Song*, a gorgeous coffee-table book with stunning images and a fascinating account of their journey.)

As the sun set over the river, we stood on the muddy shoreline. From time to time, we walked knee-deep into the water to better position the boat as the couple tried to shoot the perfect image. We hoped for a shot that would inspire people to care about the Chattahoochee, learn her history, and explore her many offerings. Still clear are my memories of the light on the water, the laughter as we tried to stand in the deep, squishy mud, and the stories we told, cementing friendships and river connections.

Thick paper guidebooks, like *The Riverkeeper's Guide*, have been replaced by smaller, more functional waterproof books that can be taken on a river for immediate consultation. The excellent *Chattahoochee River User's Guide* by Joe Cook, in such a format, was published by Georgia

River Network and the University of Georgia Press in 2014; it's one in a series of similar guides about other Georgia rivers.

Many outdoor enthusiasts rely only on the information provided by little black screens, but I don't believe everything you need to know can be learned—or the directions entirely trusted—from such devices. Call me old-fashioned. I still like to feel the heft of our original *Riverkeeper's Guide* in my hands, remembering the people and places described as I thumb through it randomly and read a page or look at a map.

Knowledge, adventure, and friendships. So much comes from loving a river and wanting to tell her story in the best possible way.

CHAPTER 4

Messing About in Boats

May 29, 2019

The boat is safer anchored at the port; but that's not the aim of boats.
—*Paulo Coelho*

It is dusk when I start down the Cabin Creek trail on this evening in late May. The walk through the woods to the river is different this time, quiet, but for the squirrels racing up and down trees, and a bit gloomy. I walk quickly in the darkening forest tunnel, noticing few flowers anywhere, except for the fly poison, whose blooms are beginning to turn pale green.

The Chattahoochee is very low. Its current is drifting slowly downstream, around dozens of exposed rocks. The river's geology—its bony skeleton—is on full display. The early evening light on the water is glorious, stimulating all my senses. I walk into the river, jumping onto the rock slabs that jut up from the water at angles like frozen waves. They are an example of foliation, according to my friend Bill Witherspoon, coauthor of *Roadside Geology of Georgia*.

Subsurface pressures imprinted this foliation into the rock about 350 million years ago, squeezing minerals within metamorphic rock to create sheet-like structures. Later forces shoved the rock up onto the continent, rotating the foliation to a southeast tilt. Now, they are my frozen waves.

After many years working on and beside the river, I feel as though I'm relating to her in an even more intimate way—perhaps more than at any other time during my two decades of riverkeeping. Is it because I no longer have a responsibility to investigate, defend, and testify on the river's behalf? Is it because my river outings are no longer driven by the need for outcomes, other than pleasure? Or because I have slowed down and become more attentive? Probably, all of the above. No matter the reasons, my meanderings and the memories they evoke are immensely satisfying.

With the workday over, quite a few boaters float past me in canoes, kayaks, and rafts. Two young men relax in a boat with a portable player that sends music over the shoals and to the shore. I perch on my sitting rock, watching the flowing tableau and remembering many of my own adventures in various watercraft on the Chattahoochee.

An Old Town canoe that had seen better days was donated to River-keeper in the organization's first year to serve as a patrol boat. I used it occasionally to explore the river and its tributaries but quickly realized that we needed a faster watercraft. We needed a boat that could easily go upstream as well as down. While we sought our own boat, we hitched rides with friends on their motorboats.

A fishing guide who had just started a business on the river in the na-tional park agreed to help us investigate an old landfill beside the river, downstream of Atlanta's water treatment plant. Alice Champagne—my first employee and exceptional righthand assistant for many years—and a graduate student intern joined us on board the small boat. The trip would require passing over and coming back through a low weir (dam). Large rocks had been placed in the river to create the weir to slow down and pool water immediately upstream at the city's water intake pump for easier withdrawal.

A highly capable boatman in national park waters, our fishing guide and captain had never motored through this tricky weir downstream of the national park. It included a not-insignificant drop and—as we learned the hard way—demanded enough water and a lightweight boat running on plane (with the bow lifted over its wave) for successful passage. We made it down the man-made structure, collected a sample of the smelly water seeping from the landfill, and started back upstream.

With four of us in the boat and not enough speed to lift the bow, we made it only halfway up the weir before the boat sank like a rock in the chilly, early spring water. Swimming, our captain followed his sinking boat downstream. The rest of us dog-paddled to an island, the nearest shore. I held the landfill water sample over my head, trying to keep it safe. What to do? The river was moving too fast and was too cold for us to safely swim from the island to the shore.

I called my mother-in-law on my cell phone, which had been protected in my dry bag, and asked her to pick my sons up from school. I explained that I was stranded on an island in the middle of the river. Not surpris-ingly, she laughed and then agreed to help.

Who could we call to retrieve us from the island in this limited-access, industrial section of the river? I thought about Georgia Power's Plant McDonough-Atkinson located a mile downstream. They had a boat! The plant employees with whom I spoke were surprised but generously agreed to help us get off the island.

As we waited for our rescuers, the graduate student worried that the media might get wind of our predicament. We could see the headline in bold, black type: "Riverkeeper rescued after sinking boat." Not a good look for our first year in operation. Fortunately, we were spared this indignity. Also, luckily, the good people at the city's water treatment plant had a winch to pull our friend's water-logged boat up the riverbank to safety.

Later that same year, a boat with a jet drive motor was donated to Riverkeeper; it was perfect for our shallow, rocky river. Using an engine to power a strong water pump, and with no propeller extending below the hull, the jet allowed passage over obstacles that could restrict access to other propeller-driven outboard boats. Serendipitously, an experienced boat captain—also a geologist, catfish noodler, dulcimer maker, and all-around unique individual—named Harlan Trammell moved home to Atlanta from the Florida Keys.

Harlan had read about our work in the local paper. He volunteered to operate and maintain our new boat, ultimately working on staff for Riverkeeper for nearly fourteen years. With his outstanding skills on the water and loyalty to our cause, Harlan made valuable contributions to our efforts before he moved back to the Keys.

In 2005, ten years after the sinking boat episode, Atlanta mayor Shirley Franklin was running for her second term. She asked if we could take her and the city's watershed commissioner on the river in our patrol boat. She wanted to see, firsthand, the condition of the Chattahoochee within the city. Before we embarked, the mayor's presswoman gave her a waterproof camera to document the trip.

The river was high and filled with urban debris that day—the sort of trash that flows off streets, parking lots, and industrial sites when it rains, and into the nearest waterway. As usual, plastic items of varying size floated alongside us as we traveled downstream.

Suddenly, the jet drive motor sputtered; something had been sucked into the device. After pulling over to the riverbank and anchoring, Harlan jumped into the water. As the mayor, her security detail, the commissioner, and I watched, he took the motor apart. A tiny piece of plastic was found to be the culprit, removed, and presented to the mayor as a souvenir. We were soon on our way; however, our adventures for that day were not yet over.

Motoring back upstream, we decided to investigate the land-clearing activity we had noticed earlier on our way downstream. Harlan slowed the boat as we approached the spot where bulldozers were cutting down trees and shrubs to the edge of the riverbank; some plants and dirt were falling into the river.

The mayor took pictures of what appeared to be a violation of the state law that protects the riparian vegetative buffers that help keep our waterways clean. One of Riverkeeper's top priorities has been to strengthen and secure the enforcement of this important environmental law.

After the boat trip, Mayor Franklin held up her camera and announced to the gathering of media and friends that she was giving it to me to find out what was going on with the land-clearing. A curious reporter followed me as I drove to the site. I assumed we would find a private developer who unintentionally—or perhaps purposefully—had violated the buffer protection law. Instead, we learned that Georgia Power, the state's dominant electric utility, was behind the destruction, being of the opinion, we were later told, that they were exempt from the stream buffer laws because "that's the way it has always been."

I called Bert Langley—an ecologist, wooden boatbuilder, and one of the best environmental managers at the Georgia Environmental Protection Division (EPD)—and explained the situation. I had worked collaboratively with Bert, then the head of the state's emergency response program, many times over the years. He inspected the site, immediately understood the problem, and took appropriate action.

Several major news stories later, including one that, tongue-in-cheek, called the mayor an "environmental whistleblower," Georgia Power finally agreed to restore the riverbank and comply with the water protection law at all of its projects statewide—just like everyone else clearing land near a river, stream, or lake.

Riverkeepers must have boats, of course, and ours have played a huge role in our work to protect the Chattahoochee over nearly thirty years. Thanks to generous supporters, our fleet has grown from one old canoe to a jet drive patrol boat (our third is in operation today), a large catamaran, two lake pontoon boats (one can carry more than forty passengers), and dozens of kayaks and canoes.

A great blue heron (*Ardea herodias*), the largest and most widespread North American heron, stands on the banks of the Chattahoochee River. Photo: Tom Wilson.

CHAPTER 5

Where Did the Animals and Birds Go?

June 5, 2019

My friend Cynthia Patterson, a longtime national park volunteer, joins me at Cabin Creek today. Almost immediately, we notice that shrubs and small trees along the trail have been "pruned," apparently by someone who has not been trained or authorized by the National Park Service. Rather than making cuts at branch nodes, and then tossing them into the woods to clear the trail, the pruner has snipped and sawed indiscriminatingly. Branches have been dropped into the path and the creek. Thankfully, nature will eventually triumph over the shoddy work of humans.

In disturbed areas along the trail and in low-lying, wet patches, we find an invader from Asia. It's Japanese stiltgrass (*Microstegium vimineum*): an annual grass once used as a packing material that is one of the most damaging invasive plant species in the eastern U.S. Infestations spread rapidly and the seeds—as many as 1,000 per plant—can remain viable in soil for years. First noticed a hundred years ago in this country, stiltgrass is spread primarily by water. It also attaches to animals and humans, hence the proximity to well-traveled trails.

I show Cynthia the native fly poison plants and their blooms, which are much greener than a week ago. We find a native black cohosh (*Actaea racemosa*) nearby, also blooming with white flowers; the roots and stems of this plant have been used for centuries to reduce hot flashes during menopause. As the seasons unfold, I anticipate learning more about the biotic treasures on this rich, woodland slope.

Walking upstream along the river, we're surprised to find a large chestnut oak tree (*Quercus prinus*) fallen across the trail. With no observable gaping hole in the ground, its origin is a mystery—until we look up to the rocky outcrop above the trail. The sizable tree had found a home on the very edge of the rocks in small pockets of soil, but gravity had finally prevailed. It was likely aided by the severe droughts in recent years, when trees are weakened by reduced growth.

Because the river is low, it's easy to see piles of freshwater clam shells (*Corbicula fluminea*) on the shore, eaten, we assume, by native muskrats (*Ondatra zibethicus*). These invasive mollusks from Asia can be found throughout the Americas and elsewhere. Cynthia shows me holes in the riverbank near the shells. They indicate muskrat burrows where the animals can make a quick retreat, if discovered while eating. Such clever little creatures that may let me see them one day.

These muskrats are fortunate to have found a home within a protected national park, where they are less likely to be disturbed or harmed. On private land, and some public land, human activities can destroy prime wildlife habitat. Too often, the damage is caused by ignorance and apathy, bolstered by a profit motive. During a boat outing many years ago, the questions from a young passenger gave me a fresh perspective on all that is lost when natural habitats are damaged or destroyed.

A young girl climbed onto our pontoon boat with her father and sister for a cruise on a small lake created more than a hundred years ago. In 1904 the Chattahoochee was dammed by Georgia Power to produce hydropower to run Atlanta's trolley cars. I expected the six-year-old passenger to be a bit shy, possibly overwhelmed by the adventure. She wasn't in the least.

Her perky British accent surprised me when she began to speak, but her questions astonished me. "How was the boat fueled; did it pollute the air; and how did the motor work? What sort of fish lived in the lake; what did they eat; and how were they affected by pollution? Why had the river been dammed and how did that affect fish?" She seemed to already know the answers and just wanted confirmation.

We rounded a bend in the narrow lake that, when the dam was built, had flooded substantial rapids and a thirty-five-foot waterfall. Originally called Bull Sluice, the name given to the rapids by Cherokees, the dam and lake were later renamed Morgan Falls to recognize, in the modern way, their primary financial investor.

An ugly clear-cut could be seen on the shoreline ahead; every tree and plant had been removed on the steep hill sloping down to the lake. Eroding gullies, stained bright orange with red clay, were visible where wildlife had once thrived in a stable environment.

According to my friend Alan Toney—one of the original "river rats" who helped create the Chattahoochee River National Recreation Area— the forested area next to the water once teemed with wildlife. In the winter, hundreds of songbirds, including warblers, foraged in and around an ancient stand of bamboo and its invasive companions: kudzu and wisteria. Further upslope, huge native pines, oaks, and other mature species had provided excellent habitat. No longer.

I knew that the gash on the hillside had been created by Sandy Springs, a city in Atlanta's northern suburbs, but this was my first view of the clear-cut. Local officials wanted a park, specifically a dog park, they said. They apparently wanted it so badly and quickly that they "forgot" to secure any environmental permits.

Permitting could have safeguarded the buffer land next to the water, imposed conditions on upslope grading and construction to minimize erosion impacts, and required a revegetation with long-term maintenance. The city would still have a park.

It was apparent to many observers that the city simply didn't want to bother with the paperwork and processing time required with permitting. Presumably, city officials expected that they could ask for, and receive, forgiveness later. By then, the entire site would have been cleared.

As much as I love dogs, all I could think of was a slightly revised version of Joni Mitchell's song about paving paradise and putting up a parking lot. In this case, putting up a parking lot for dog owners and a playground for dogs. Once "great views" of the lake were created with every tree and plant removed from the hillside, the city decided to build Morgan Falls Overlook Park, now a highly manicured people park. The dogs were forced to play elsewhere.

The little girl stared, and I waited to see what she would say. A simple question with a complicated answer: "Why did someone do that?" Followed by: "Where did all the animals and birds go?" Indeed, where did all those wonderful, clever, and important critters go?

I don't remember what I said, but I'm sure that my answer wasn't very satisfactory to this intelligent, empathetic young girl. She must be college age now. I wonder what she's doing and if she's still asking important questions. My bet is yes. It's young people like her who will help us find more sustainable ways forward with smart decisions that respect all life.

Based on complaints filed by Riverkeeper and others, Sandy Springs was put on temporary probation for violating environmental protection laws—an act that mandated greater oversight by state agencies of the city's development activities affecting waterways. The city was also required to restore some of the riparian buffer with trees and shrubs, as mitigation for the damage. The wildlife habitat that had been half a century or more in the making was gone, forever.

CHAPTER 6

Newt, Cynthia, and Atlanta Sewers

June 12, 2019

Water is the driving force of all nature.
—Leonardo da Vinci

After a weekend of torrential summer rain, on the heels of a long dry spell, I head to Cabin Creek with city friends Lucie Langford Canfield and Alice Franklin, expecting a high, muddy river. We are not disappointed. The intense storms have transformed the trail; it is slick and bright orange where the Georgia red clay, colored by iron oxide, is exposed. The wind and rain have toppled small trees and ripped leaves from branches. There are small gullies along the trail, highlighting the need for water bars or dikes to slow the runoff.

We pick our way carefully downhill among the roots and slippery ground. Lucie and Alice are impressed with the richness of the forest, so close to the city and literally a quarter of a mile from wealthy neighborhoods. An accomplished photographer, Lucie takes dozens of photos, documenting the intricate patterns made by vines, nests, lichen, moss, and cracks in the rock outcrops.

We examine the fly poison and discuss its many benefits. Other than birds, we see no wildlife in the damp woods or on the turbulent river. Cabin Creek and its tributaries are flowing with greater volume than usual, but the water is clear, thanks to the eighty-acre, forested watershed that drains into them. In this largely undeveloped landscape, when the ground is bombarded by raindrops, trees, plants, and decomposing material on the forest floor help hold the soil in place.

As expected, the Chattahoochee is pumpkin colored. Construction activities near the river and its tributaries that are missing adequate erosion control measures and riverbank sloughing from water releases at Buford Dam have taken their toll on the river. The trail along the Chattahoochee is flooded in several places, so we take side paths to avoid the new shoreline and large puddles. The river hurries past us with impressive rapids. White, foamy crests are the visual evidence of rocky shoals below.

Muddy river water is not just unsightly; it can also be dangerous. Contaminants, such as chemical waste, heavy metals, pesticides, and untreated sewage, flow into waterways in the storm runoff from construction and industrial sites—and from roads, roof tops, parking lots, broken sewer lines, and manholes. The pollutants are often attached to fast-moving dirt particles. When sewer systems are not regularly maintained and repaired, sewage can also spill into streams—even when it's not raining—due to reduced capacity in the underground pipes and the proximity of these gravity lines to waterways.

The Chattahoochee River downstream of Atlanta was considered one of the most polluted waterways in Georgia, when Riverkeeper was established in 1994. It was disgusting, hazardous, and shameful. A friend who worked at a power plant on the river in the 1980s remembers seeing condoms floating downstream; he and his buddies called them "Chattahoochee whitefish." The city regularly bypassed untreated and partially treated sewage and polluted stormwater into the river at least three to four times per month in the 1990s—and had been doing so for many years.

This intolerable negligence affected waterways throughout metro Atlanta and the river itself downstream to West Point Lake, the drinking water source for the city of LaGrange. Located seventy miles southwest of the metro region, the reservoir was described in a front-page, *Atlanta Journal-Constitution* article, in 1988, as dying from algal blooms (the rapid growth of microscopic algae) caused by an oversupply of nutrients: phosphates in laundry detergent and untreated sewage.

David Bayne, a biologist with Auburn University who had studied the lake from the time it filled in the mid-1970s, was quoted in a news article, saying: "If West Point Lake were a human, it would be very obese, and all the vital signs would be pointing to a very early death."

Former state representative Wade Milam, a Democrat from LaGrange who worked tirelessly for years to protect the reservoir near his home, said: "We were told it would be a dead lake in ten years, if we didn't do something." In 1989 it was estimated that nearly four million tons of phosphorus were flowing down the Chattahoochee and into West Point Lake every year.

Milam led the legislative effort to pass a statewide ban on phosphates in laundry detergent in 1990 to reduce nutrient loads. He prevailed over the bitter opposition of lobbyists for detergent manufacturers. Several years later, he became a key partner in Riverkeeper's work to stop Atlanta's chronic sewage overflows that were contributing to nutrient and bacterial pollution of West Point Lake. (The state had imposed a phosphorus limit on permitted releases, or discharges, from Atlanta's sewer plants in 1991, but the city failed to comply by the deadlines imposed. Opposition from neighborhood activists over the chosen engineering solution was a major factor.)

Atlanta's chronic mismanagement of its sewer infrastructure and the system's deteriorating condition had been documented for years in government reports and water monitoring data collected by various entities. A study completed by a blue-ribbon commission in 1990 was particularly alarming, but the final report was never released to the public. The study found evidence of major problems, notably one hundred sewer cave-ins in the city during a single year; one involved a hook and ladder fire truck that dropped into a sewer.

The sewer crisis also resulted in deaths. In 1993, a year before Riverkeeper was established, several major storms overwhelmed a seventy-year-old stormwater pipe under the Marriott Courtyard Hotel parking lot in midtown Atlanta. The huge pipe collapsed, bringing the lot down with it. Two people died. A young woman and her car fell 35 feet into the 200-foot-diameter sinkhole, along with a hotel worker who was in the lot at dawn looking for someone to jump-start his car. Several empty vehicles also fell into the sinkhole. One was found plugging a large drainage pipe, three miles away from the hotel.

This disaster forced the city to finally accelerate the repair of its decaying infrastructure by funding studies and some pipe replacements, but the plans were slow to be implemented. They were also inadequate for the magnitude of the crisis. Then-mayor Bill Campbell and his staff repeatedly said it would be too expensive to fix the entire system. The city paid the daily fines imposed by the state in the 1990s, which ultimately totaled more than $20 million. At the same time, Campbell freely admitted that the penalties cost the city less than the price of overhauling the system.

During the early 1990s, debates over Atlanta's strategies for meeting government mandates to fix the sewer system were intense among elected officials, city leaders, engineers, and neighborhood activists. The arguments led to major program design and facility siting changes, construction delays, substantial fines, bans on new sewer hookups for development, and poor relationships with downstream communities. An analysis by Research Atlanta, Inc. called the situation "a near paralysis of public decision-making."

From the moment we opened the Riverkeeper office in 1994 and began our work, we knew what our first, major challenge would be. We had to aggressively tackle the biggest, but certainly not the only, pollution source in the Chattahoochee River watershed: the chronic spills from the Atlanta sewage system. These filthy overflows had plagued the river and its tributaries for decades.

After meeting with downstream leaders long concerned about the city's pollution and its effect on their economies and health, a Riverkeeper-led coalition hired environmental attorney David Pope. Our group included seven local governments and associations, two private landowners, and a downstream river conservation group. In May 1995, we sent a letter to Mayor Campbell, copying state and federal regulatory agencies; it outlined the city's violations of the federal Clean Water Act and asked for a response. We never received one.

As our frustration with the city's political posturing and inability to deal with the longtime crisis mounted, our coalition decided it was time to take the matter into an entirely new arena: the federal court system. Based on their record, we lacked any faith that the Georgia Environmental Protection Division would take the necessary enforcement actions against the city. Atlanta would have to be forced to overhaul its sewer system in a comprehensive and timely manner.

In the summer of 1995, our coalition of public and private entities sent a letter to Atlanta, EPD, and the U.S. EPA, putting them on notice of the city's pollution violations; the letter was required by the citizen suit provision of the federal Clean Water Act. Again, no one responded.

With no other choice, our plaintiff's group filed a lawsuit against the city in October 1995, less than a year before the Olympic Games were scheduled to open in Atlanta. This bold but essential move dominated my riverkeeping career. It was strongly supported by the Riverkeeper board under Rutherford Seydel's leadership. Citizen lawsuits brought by individuals or nonprofits like Riverkeeper have greatly improved the enforcement of environmental laws throughout the country over the past four decades. Government agencies are too often pressured by elected officials and their campaign donors not to enforce the law.

The journey was not an easy one; however, the results were more than worth the effort. Riverkeeper's lawsuit and subsequent settlement have yielded significant results for the river, the city and its neighborhoods, and downstream communities.

In early 1997, as our lawsuit was grinding through the court system, John Hankinson—the head of EPA's regional office in Atlanta, an environmental attorney, and a locally beloved blues harmonica player—decided to involve his agency. He wanted to help bring the city into compliance and clean up the river.

Hankinson used EPA's legal authority and engineering staff to make unannounced inspections at sewage plants and walk many miles along the streams in the city that parallel gravity sewer lines. The system failures and high levels of fecal contamination in the urban streams were more egregious than anyone expected. I remember his phone call to me after the major investigation, in which he offered EPA's help.

Hankinson suggested that his agency join our lawsuit and provide the new evidence of significant, ongoing violations to help us resolve the matter in a holistic manner—in other words, demand that the city's entire sewer system be overhauled to meet water quality standards by specific dates. If we prevailed in court, negotiated agreements would be outlined in a legally binding consent decree. Before moving forward, Hankinson asked if we could provide him with evidence of bipartisan support. It would help convince his superiors in Washington that he was taking an appropriate legal action against a major southern city.

In 1996 I had been asked to join a new environmental advisory committee created by then–House Speaker Newt Gingrich, a Georgian who had once represented the district downstream of Atlanta. He was intimately familiar with the Chattahoochee and Atlanta's sewer problems. In fact, after the *Atlanta Journal-Constitution* reported on the city's pollution of the river and West Point Lake in 1988, then-congressman Gingrich called a meeting with state and federal environmental officials. He wanted to discuss the matter and his concerns.

Several people urged me to decline the request, given the Republican Speaker's polarizing political record. I decided to join the committee, thinking he might be willing to support our work on the Chattahoochee. If he refused, I would have a story to tell anyone interested. Working through his staff, I asked the Speaker to send a letter to the EPA, urging the agency to take a tougher stance on the city's chronic sewage spills. Gingrich's office agreed.

Needing a progressive voice to add to Gingrich's conservative one, I thought of Representative Cynthia McKinney: a Democrat, outspoken liberal activist, and the first African American woman from Georgia to serve in Congress. My younger son, Robert, was on the same soccer team as her son and they were friends. One evening at soccer practice, as we sat together watching our boys, I made my pitch. She said she was happy to help.

A few weeks later, a startling headline appeared in the *Atlanta Journal-Constitution*: "Dear EPA: McKinney, Gingrich Agree." The article continued: "Two people who rarely see eye to eye, U.S. Rep. Cynthia McKinney and House Speaker Newt Gingrich, agree on at least one thing: Atlanta hasn't done enough to fix its sewage problems." A neighborhood leader was quoted in the article, saying: "It takes sewage to make these two agree on something."

The EPA's John Hankinson had the necessary political support to join our litigation against the city and help bring it to a successful conclusion with his agency's legal authority and technical expertise. I had learned an important lesson. Never discount the possibility that those who disagree with you in most instances might come to your aid in some instances. In other words, it never hurts to ask for help. You just might get it.

The Chattahoochee River within the Chattahoochee River National Recreation Area has been named one of the top one hundred trout streams in the United States. It is one of only three trout rivers in the world that runs through a metropolitan area of a million or more people. Photo: Tom Wilson.

CHAPTER 7

One of the Best Trout Streams in America

June 19, 2019

> Many men go fishing all of their lives without knowing
> that it is not fish they are after.
> —*Henry David Thoreau*

I am back on the trail on my own for the first time in several weeks and it's a wonderful feeling. When I'm alone and not distracted by companions—however much I enjoy showing them my special place—I always feel more a part of the woods and water.

An intense storm during the previous week caused significant erosion on the road into the park. The National Park Service had blocked my usual parking spot with tree trunks to keep cars out of the gullies. Despite the storm, the creeks are not as full as they were on my last visit and the water is clear. Mushrooms have popped up in many places: a lovely orange specimen, white mushrooms on a fallen mountain laurel branch, and tiny bright orange mushrooms. Dark green Christmas ferns (*Polystichum acrostichoides*) are noticeable along the entire trail.

For the first time, I hear the buzzing and clicking sound of the insects that, to me, will always announce the arrival of summer. Cicadas! They bring a flood of childhood memories of warm, humid, school-free days. Attempting to attract a mate, male cicadas produce an exceptionally loud song from vibrating membranes in their abdomens. These organs, called tymbals, create varying sounds among the more than three thousand cicada species.

Annual cicadas are also called dog-day cicadas as in the dog days of summer, when Sirius, the Dog Star, aligns with the sun in July and August and cicada singing is particularly loud. Periodical cicadas emerge simultaneously from the ground every thirteen or seventeen years: the longest life cycle of any insect on earth. This evolutionary strategy has allowed the insects to persist for at least forty million and possibly two hundred million years. Once the soil temperature at a depth of eight inches reaches about sixty-four degrees, the cicadas crawl out of the ground. Tree roots sustain them during their time underground: a few years for annual cicadas and thirteen or seventeen years for periodical cicadas.

After escaping their subterranean homes, the cicadas find vertical structures—a tree, shrub, or building—and climb as high as ten feet before shedding their exoskeletons. They escape the hard shells through a tiny slit in their backs and unfold large, transparent wings.

In 2011 Georgia's only hatch of thirteen-year cicadas, members of the Great Southern Brood, appeared in the middle of the state. That summer, I paddled up Long Cane Creek with Jason Ulseth, then Riverkeeper's technical programs director and now the riverkeeper. The stream meanders through Troup County before entering the Chattahoochee below West Point Dam. As our kayaks moved slowly up the creek, we were increasingly surrounded by the overpowering humming and buzzing of thousands of male cicadas in the dense tree canopy above us. They were singing to establish territory and attract females.

Walking the Cabin Creek trail on mid-to-late summer evenings, I also hear the staccato chirping of the large, grasshopper-like katydids (*Tettigoniidae*) or bush crickets. Both sexes produce their distinctive songs (*katy-did . . . katy-didn't*) by rubbing their forewings together.

Author and environmental scientist Rachel Carson appreciated these powerful, life-affirming sounds. She wrote in the late 1940s: "'What do you know about insect voices?' I suddenly demanded one August night of a friend far better versed in insect lore than I. . . . And so, began what has been one of the most fascinating and satisfying of all my interests in the world of nature." Remembering later the "little world" into which she'd stepped the previous summer, Carson recalled "a sudden awakened curiosity about those insect voices that I had heard—and yet not heard—all my life."

The river is lower than last week, but still a little muddy with some visible rocks. I take a closer look at the small, stone bridge over Cabin Creek, which is covered with plants. On my next visit, I'll clear away some of the vines. As I walk upstream, I expect to find the downed chestnut oak but be able to walk underneath its large branches. Unfortunately, the tree has settled more in the previous week. It is completely blocking the trail, so I turn back and send another report to busy park staff and trail volunteers.

On the way back up the trail, I notice tiny, bright orange mushrooms on the streambank at an elbow in Cabin Creek. A few inches away from the fungi, I see quick movement in the water. Tiny fish—the first I've seen on my walks—are darting about. Could they possibly be trout fry? Have they hatched in the creek, where they can grow and hide from predators before swimming downstream to the big water?

The Chattahoochee has been named one of the best trout streams in the United States. Only three trout rivers in the world run through a metropolitan region of a million or more people. Prior to the construction of Buford Dam, the river was a warmwater fishery. Today, it's called a tailwater fishery, one that exists solely because of the influence of an upstream dam. Cold water stored at the bottom of a man-made reservoir like Lake Lanier is released into the river below its dam, creating trout habitat. While native brook trout (*Salvelinus fontinalis*) can be found in the mountain streams of the Chattahoochee's headwaters, the city portion of the river below Buford Dam is home to nonnative rainbow (*Oncorhynchus mykiss*) and brown (*Salmo trutta*) trout.

Originally stocked by the state starting in the 1970s, these trout species are now reproducing naturally, as documented for more than two decades. To meet the heavy demand of Atlanta area anglers, rainbows continue to be stocked. No brown trout have been introduced since 2005, yet the river seems to be full of them. In 2014 a state-record brown was caught within the Chattahoochee River National Recreation Area; it measured 31.5 inches long and weighed 20 pounds and 14 ounces.

Given their urban location, most of the tributaries to the Chattahoochee in metro Atlanta have poor water quality. The culprits are storm runoff carrying thermal pollution from hot pavement, chemicals from lawns and landscaping, and eroded soil from construction sites. Physical changes to urban stream channels from the rapid and extreme flow of high water (called flashiness) further damage waterways near dense development.

Despite these insults, in the mid-2000s, biologists with the state and several federal agencies documented rainbow trout reproduction in a handful of warmwater tributaries to the Chattahoochee. These streams boasted largely forested watersheds and ample vegetated buffers that keep water quality and temperature suitable for egg incubation. Cabin Creek is one of the tributaries where prespawning males and females were found.

I have fished in freshwater and saltwater, but without the patience or skill needed for the sport, I prefer to watch others throw their lines into the water while I enjoy the sights, sounds, and smells that come with spending time in a boat. Memories of two fishing trips on the Chattahoochee River remain strong, though they occurred decades ago.

A thirty-five-mile stretch of the Chattahoochee from Buford Dam to Morgan Falls Dam in north Atlanta was designated a seasonal trout stream for many years. This means the river was closed to fishing from late fall to early spring to protect the fishery and increase angler success. On an opening day in the mid-1990s, I joined Bill Couch, the manager of the state's Buford Trout Hatchery on the river.

I had gotten up early and driven upstream from the city in the dark. As my eyes adjusted to the dim light in the thick mist over the river, I could see dozens of people quietly moving into their boats. Each had a rod in hand, ready to test the waters that had been off limits for nearly half a year.

Bill helped me into his boat and we paddled slowly into the middle of the stream. As I watched, the people around us baited their hooks and dropped their lines. Within minutes, they began pulling trout into their boats. I wasn't lucky with any fish that day, but it didn't matter. I had seen the pure joy that overcomes people of all ages, especially the young, when they pull handsome, wiggling fish out of clean, cold water. That was more than enough.

Not long after I experienced the opening day of trout season, I was invited by Gandy Glover—the colorful former mayor of Newnan, Georgia, and an expert fisherman—to explore a rural stretch of the Chattahoochee. It was many miles downstream of the trout waters in the national park. At the confluence of Centralhatchee Creek and the river, near Franklin, Georgia, Gandy caught a hybrid striped bass: a silvery, spiny-rayed fish with horizontal streaks on its sides.

As it thrashed around in his hands, Gandy opened the fish's mouth expertly and urged me to feel the tongue before he released it back to the river. Without hesitating, I put my finger in its mouth. I felt the sandpaper-like tooth patch that grows on the back of its tongue and is used to grip prey. Making this physical connection with the fish, communicating by touch in such an unusual way, embedded an exceptional memory. It also reinforced for me the many ways we humans can relate to other species. Like ourselves, they too depend on the gift that is the Chattahoochee River.

The people who fish the Chattahoochee are among her best defenders. They understand how eroding soil and damaged stream buffers can harm water quality and habitat for trout, warmwater fish, and other aquatic species. During my riverkeeping years, I loved speaking to fishing groups about the issues facing the river. Working with these anglers in schools, at the state legislature, and, when necessary, in the courts was always a pleasure. Our goals were the same: clean, accessible waterways for everyone.

CHAPTER 8
A Free Press Saves Rivers

June 26, 2019

When I arrive at the park in the late afternoon, I encounter a group of university students at the trailhead. They are looking at the East Palisades map, trying to determine how they had missed the overlook deck with its grand view of the river. I show them and then check an old drainpipe discarded nearby.

The week before, I had found and removed multiple plastic bags of dog waste from the pipe. I left a note asking park visitors to please bag and bin the bacteria-laden material in the future. I find my note crumpled under a large plastic bag of dog waste with unbagged waste crowning the mess. It was difficult, though not impossible, to remove it all. Was someone sending me a (very unpleasant) message? I hope not.

With trash bag and trekking pole in hand, I head down the trail, noting that the path has again been scoured by recent storms; the downhill trail has become a chute for fast-moving water. Like just about every other trail in the national park, this one should be repaired or realigned. Meager park budgets in recent decades have made such projects unlikely without help from private donors and nonprofit organizations.

The forest is dimming, and as dusk approaches, I see, to my amazement, a blinking lightning bug. The iconic beetle of summer is apparently ready for night to arrive. I breathe deeply, trying to let go of the city, traffic, and the busyness in my head. Breathing in nature and restoring some peace of mind, I appreciate all that the forest and streams have to give.

Botanist and nature writer Robin Wall Kimmerer explains the symbiotic relationship between humans and our green world in these beautiful words: "The breath of plants gives life to animals and the breath of animals gives life to plants. My breath is your breath, your breath is mine. It's the great poem of give and take, of reciprocity that animates the world."

I'm able to turn off my internal voices, finally, and focus on the sounds outside my head: the cicadas buzzing and clicking, the scampering noises of small animals, and the wind singing in the leaves. The air is muggy, heavy with moisture. More mushrooms have emerged from the leafy forest floor since my last visit.

As I approach the river, the air I inhale is cooler. A foggy mist floats above the water, creating a gauze-like curtain that renders the scene ethereal and mysterious. The fog is the result of warm, moist air flowing over the cold water released from the depths of Lake Lanier through Buford Dam. My spirits are immediately uplifted. I hear the voices before I see their boats. Canoes, kayaks, and floating inner tubes carry river adventurers through the mist. My photos document the beauty, but they tell only a part of the story. Missing are the sounds, pungent smells, and pockets of cool air.

The chestnut oak, which had fallen several weeks before, has been cut and moved off the trail. I can once again proceed upriver. There, I find two young men taking photos of young women clad in jungle attire with the bright green bamboo shoots as backdrop. After a quick look at the river, I head back up the trail. Along the way, I notice a blackberry vine next to a large pine tree. Hopefully, I'll find berries on my next visit.

Unfailingly, these walks along the river help revive me. I rarely forget, however, that the beauty I'm able to enjoy in this national park—a forever-protected landscape—is just a few miles upstream of the industrial section of the river: a place with a different ambience, where the wastes from our daily lives in the city and its industrial processes find a repository.

In the 1990s, before Riverkeeper and our partners could help stop the city's chronic sewage spills and other pollution, we had to find ways to communicate the grim nature of the environmental problem. We needed to garner support for what would clearly be a huge and expensive undertaking: the overhaul of the city's massive sewage system. The media and its correspondents played a critical role in this endeavor.

It was supposed to be a routine boat trip for a reporter who wanted to see our threatened river. In the pre–boat ride interview, we found that Bill Schulz already knew a great deal about the Chattahoochee's recent history. He had done a good job of researching the pollution crisis, including Riverkeeper's lawsuit against the city of Atlanta for its sewer system failures.

It was midsummer 1996 and hot as we launched our boat at a ramp in the industrial section of the river. We motored upstream past landfills, a sand-dredging operation, and the city's R. M. Clayton sewage treatment facility; today, it's known, euphemistically, as a water reclamation plant. At the time processing about eighty million gallons of wastewater per day, the eighty-five-year-old Clayton plant is still the largest sewage facility in the Southeast.

Our trip tracked the usual tour until Harlan and I saw something strange ahead. Brownish water was bubbling up from the surface of the river near the Clayton plant, but not at the location where the facility is permitted to discharge its treated wastewater. Suddenly, the flow subsided, just as mysteriously as it had begun.

I got out of the boat onto a small mud island full of tires, cans, and other trash, exposed because of extremely low water levels. When Bill saw me struggling with little success to remove an embedded tire, he got out of our boat to help. Together, we maneuvered the heavy rubber doughnut into the boat, getting covered with filth in the process. Then, we heard a loud grating sound. Brownish, smelly water bubbled up again. This time the flow was immense. We scrambled back into the boat as the island was inundated with a flood of untreated sewage.

The investigation that followed my call to city officials to report the spill, and the subsequent news stories, revealed that we had encountered an accidental discharge of eight hundred thousand gallons of untreated sewage into the river from the Clayton plant. A city employee had decided to test a gate—to see if it was working properly—in an area of the plant where releases were allowed only during extreme emergencies. When the gate was raised, the untreated sewage flowed directly into the Chattahoochee.

Bill's excellent story about the event appeared in newspapers throughout Georgia, serving as a graphic example of the magnitude of the problems with Atlanta's sewers and their operation. I learned later that, when he was with us, Bill had been fighting pancreatic cancer and receiving chemotherapy. He died from the disease later that year. While he lived, this tough, investigative journalist never stopped searching for ways to use the written word to help people understand the world around them, providing information that could lead to enlightenment and action.

The reporters, editorial writers, photographers, and videographers who revealed the good, bad, and ugly about the Chattahoochee for their various media outlets were essential to our early success. Without their relentless pursuit of facts and their illuminating stories and images, it would have been much harder to pressure decision makers to take action to clean up the river. It would have been much more difficult to explain to the public all that was at stake.

The *Atlanta Journal-Constitution* provided a significant amount of ink and space to the Chattahoochee and its challenges. The paper's editors allowed Charles Seabrook, Stacy Shelton, and other excellent journalists to pursue the facts and present the truth.

River otters (*Lontra canadensis*) are regularly found in the Chattahoochee, frolicking in the water, sliding, diving, and enjoying a crayfish meal. Photo: Tom Wilson

CHAPTER 9

A Water Trail and the Governor's Lake

July 27, 2019

Those who contemplate the beauty of the earth find reserves of strength that will endure as long as life lasts.
—*Rachel Carson*

I'm finally back in the Cabin Creek groove after a long road trip that included visits to a dozen national and state parks from Kentucky to Michigan and Wisconsin. There is so much protected natural beauty to experience in the United States, and many places still needing protection. As I walk slowly down the trail, deliberately listening to cicadas and summer birdsong, I contemplate all that has changed in the woods and creeks in the month that I've been gone.

Next to the trail, I notice four unusual earthen shapes in a swampy area about twenty-five feet from Cabin Creek. The little stacks look like something a child might have made with dribbled wet clay, then poked holes in the centers. Water is visible in one of the openings. I have found crayfish chimneys, built with pellets of excavated sand and mud made by the small invertebrates with their feet and mouths.

The crayfish that occupy these structures live in burrows underneath the chimneys with tunnels that are normally full of water and can extend three feet underground. With seventy species of crayfish in Georgia and no sighting of the occupants of these burrows, I can't even attempt to identify them.

They are not likely Chattahoochee crayfish (*Cambarus howardi*), which live in and near the swift waters of larger streams in the Upper Chattahoochee basin. These crustaceans, which can grow up to three inches in length, have a lavender-brown to forest green carapace (hard upper shell) decorated with red markings. I'd so love to see them. Crayfish always summon memories of the clear streams in the backyard of my childhood home.

At the river, there are pale blue flowers with bright yellow stamens on tall stems that appear to be a variety of dayflowers (*Commelina*). According to some guidebooks, they are edible and medicinal. I hear a familiar, loud humming sound coming from the river. Although I can't see it yet, it's clearly a powerboat about to come around Charlie's Island, heading upstream through the shoals. I hope that it's the Riverkeeper patrol boat, out for a cruise. It's not. So many good memories of adventures, investigations, and laughing on that boat, along with a few scares.

At the end of the trail, I find an older man sitting in a lotus position, facing the river. He tells me that his name is C.K. and that he visits the river to meditate four or five times a week. With his hands resting in his lap and a steady gaze on the flowing water, he focuses his attention on the scene before him in patient, peaceful contemplation.

I leave C.K. and begin my walk back to the trailhead, recalling places along the Chattahoochee where I have found a similar sense of tranquility through mindful attention. I think about a spot in the north Georgia mountains where the narrow river winds through a green cathedral.

The uppermost section of the Chattahoochee flows nearly fifty miles from the mountainside spring that launches the river on its way to Lake Lanier. It plunges downhill through a national forest and an alpine-themed town, past farmland, large homes, and vacation rentals. With rapids described as class II (regular waves) and a few class III (high, irregular waves), when the river is full, this is the home of Chattahoochee whitewater, rocky shoals, islands, and largely untouched natural beauty. The volume of water in the river increases with flows from mountain streams that include Sautee, Dukes, Mossy, Blue, and Flat Creeks and the Soque River.

In the mid-2000s, Riverkeeper evaluated the possibility of creating a water trail to improve recreational access for paddlers on a thirty-six-mile section of the Upper Chattahoochee—from the confluence of Sautee Creek near the town of Helen to Clarks Bridge on Lake Lanier. Paddlers have enjoyed this section of the river at least since the 1970s, when Wildwood Outfitters opened a business in the area.

Working with the rivers and trails division of the National Park Service, our report was ultimately presented to the Georgia Department of Natural Resources (DNR). The parks division of this state agency had expressed interest in creating a network of officially designated water trails. We thought that the idea of establishing an Upper Chattahoochee River water trail made sense. The state had purchased several large tracts of land along the river for future public parks.

Not everyone thought the water trail was a great idea. One politically connected landowner on the river threatened Riverkeeper with a lawsuit unless the organization stopped its study. This individual claimed that he owned the river adjacent to his property, including the water. He said that our project promoted trespass by people who would use his property as a bathroom. We didn't stop our study. He never filed a legal action. (I was told, but unable to confirm, that this landowner later influenced then–lieutenant governor Casey Cagle—a Republican with an anti-environmental record—to cause my removal from the Board of Natural Resources, a story to come.)

Riverkeeper created maps and brochures to help paddlers safely and legally access the river, working with private and public partners. Today, the Upper Chattahoochee River Water Trail is actively promoted by Georgia River Network and other nonprofits, along with local governments and ecotourism groups. The Georgia DNR has never fully embraced this water trail or any others in the state. Unfortunately, they've missed key ecotourism opportunities that have proven successful in many other states.

On a warm day in early summer 2012, we launched our patrol boat into the Chattahoochee just above Lake Lanier, where its currents begin to slow down as the river flows into the massive federal reservoir. Our destination was a place in the middle of the Upper Chattahoochee Water Trail. A water pump station was proposed at this site to feed a miles-long pipeline that would transport river water to a new, man-made reservoir called Glades, if permit applications were approved. Flat Creek, a tributary to the river, would have to be dammed for the project.

On board with us that day was a journalist with WABE, a local public radio station. He wanted to learn more about the proposed dam and reservoir project that had the strong backing of top state officials, including then-governor Nathan Deal, a Republican. Deal's longtime home is in Hall County, where the reservoir would be located. Several employees of the Georgia Environmental Protection Division, which has a role in permitting dams, told me that inside the agency they called the project "the governor's lake."

Along with area residents and environmental groups, Riverkeeper had been fighting the Glades reservoir proposal for nearly a decade. We provided technical comments to government agencies and decision makers, engaged the media, and worked with community groups. If approved, the reservoir would flood 850 acres of land and destroy eighteen miles of streams that flow into the Chattahoochee, along with forty acres of wetlands.

Under at least one scenario, the project would require siphoning massive quantities of water directly from the river at the proposed pump station to keep the new reservoir full. Projected to cost at least $350 million, the proposal was a boondoggle: a scheme to benefit real estate developers (and consultants) at the expense of taxpayers.

Described by its proponents as a public water supply reservoir, the true purpose of this controversial project was to serve as the centerpiece amenity for a massive new development on thousands of acres of timberland. This scheme was revealed more fully in previously undisclosed public documents that Riverkeeper accessed using open records laws.

The words of reservoir proponents were also damning. At an early celebratory event near the proposed dam site, boosters proclaimed the development would be "the next Peachtree City," referencing a successful, master-planned community south of the Atlanta airport. In other words, the reservoir was a private development amenity looking for a public purpose, meaning public funds and permits. Land near the proposed lake had already been rezoned for several huge mixed-use developments with more than ten thousand lots for houses.

Because of its potential impact on negotiations related to the ongoing water conflict among Georgia, Alabama, and Florida (another story to come), the proposed Glades reservoir was subject to rigorous studies by the U.S. Army Corps of Engineers. The agency's decisions could make the project a reality—or kill it.

Once completed, the Corps of Engineers' studies confirmed there was no need for additional water supply to serve the area until midcentury, if then. Among other fatal flaws, population projections for water demand had been wildly exaggerated by consultants in an attempt to justify the financing and construction of the reservoir. Even assuming a need for more water supply in the region at some future date, a far less expensive and less environmentally harmful alternative is located just downstream: Lake Lanier. By making it possible for this federal reservoir to hold more water, Lanier could serve a growing population.

The extra storage would be secured by increasing Lanier's water level by two feet above normal operating levels—to be accomplished by raising the height of several bridges over the lake and making policy and operational changes. These actions could yield an additional twenty-six billion gallons of water supply storage, equal to about five hundred million full bathtubs.

In 2016, more than fifteen years after elected officials, consultants, and lobbyists had first proposed the reservoir project, state regulators finally admitted that Glades was not viable. Consultants such as now-discredited local attorney Tommy Craig had already made significant sums from its promotion.

For years, Craig and other lobbyists had successfully worked to convince local officials, such as those in Hall County, that if they didn't start spending the millions it would take to build new water supply reservoirs, they would not be prepared for "explosive" growth. In many Georgia counties, lucrative consultant contracts created "money pits" that had to be filled by taxpayers.

More than $16 million was ultimately spent on lobbyists, lawyers, and engineering firms to study, plan, and promote the Glades scheme. In addition to Craig, the influential lobbying firm of Joe Tanner & Associates was deeply involved. Twice commissioner of the Georgia DNR, Joe Tanner founded his firm in the late 1990s, after retiring from decades with state government. Former Georgia EPD director Harold Reheis and other retired state employees joined him. The firm serves as a good example of the revolving door that allows "powerful legislators and well-placed Georgia bureaucrats" to secure "well-paid lobbying jobs," observed the *Atlanta Journal-Constitution*.

Although some Hall County officials claim that the reservoir is still on the table, it appears to be on life support. Our lengthy battle illustrates that few major environmental victories are celebrated without years of relentless persistence—and an unflagging, watchful eye toward the possible resurrection of bad ideas.

On that warm, early summer day in 2012, Jason Ulseth (at the helm), WABE reporter Jim Burress, and I motored upstream to the spot where the pump was proposed to suck more than one hundred million gallons of water per day from the river. The water would have then been piped to the new reservoir on Flat Creek to keep it full for private, waterfront homeowners. It was four years before the Glades reservoir project was finally mothballed.

It hadn't rained in some time and the river was clear and low, requiring our jet drive motorboat with its minimal draft and a skilled captain. We had both.

Arriving at the location of the proposed pump station, we slowed and then stopped our boat. Jim turned on his mic to capture the summer sounds of the forest and the flowing water that surrounded us. I don't remember how long we were quiet, attentively listening and looking, as our boat drifted in the light breeze.

What I do remember is the feeling that we were in the center of a green cathedral with dappled light entering from high windows: the few open spaces in the tree canopy. I could have remained there for hours, contemplating the natural beauty and sounds that surrounded us, building reserves of strength to carry me forward.

CHAPTER 10

National Park in the City's Backyard

August 11, 2019

National parks are the best idea we ever had.
Absolutely American, absolutely democratic, they reflect
us at our best rather than our worst.
—*Wallace Stegner*

I arrive at the trailhead parking area on this weekend morning to find it's already crowded with cars and trucks wedged into every available space—full of people anxious to spend a few hours outdoors. Again, I realize how fortunate I am to have an outstanding national park so close to my home; its more than five thousand acres in fifteen land units along forty-eight miles of river are often referred to as a "string of pearls."

The Chattahoochee River National Recreation Area is one of more than four hundred places in America that documentary filmmaker Ken Burns calls "great sections of our national landscape set aside not for kings, or the very rich, but for everyone for all time."

The forest is humid, but it feels good to be back on my trail again. Not too far down the path, I see that a huge tree, another oak, has fallen across the path, knocking down a large pine and several smaller trees. The new canopy opening will allow more sunshine to reach the forest floor.

In a forest, gaps created naturally by treefall play an important role in forest ecology by encouraging the establishment and growth of species through nutrient recycling of the tree mass. These processes are aided by the changes in space, light, moisture, and temperature. Natural disturbance can play a vital role in forest biodiversity.

Searching the treetops made more visible by this forest opening, I look for, but do not find, an interesting phenomenon called "crown shyness." Prevalent among some trees of the same species, the branches and leaves of neighbor trees do not touch each other. In these instances, the canopy displays channel-like gaps. Forest ecologists speculate that trees evolved this survival strategy to reduce the spread of harmful insects or to prevent injury from an adjacent tree during storms.

Another possibility is that the gaps preclude shading to enhance photosynthesis: the extraordinary process by which plants use sunlight, water, and carbon dioxide to create oxygen and chemical energy in the form of sugar. A concept called allelopathy suggests that neighboring trees (and other plants) may communicate using chemicals; these signals may indicate the proximity of nearby trees to slow or stop tree growth toward its neighbors.

A man in an orange vest stands beside the fallen trees with a chainsaw. He says that he likes to help clear and manage the park trails near his home. I doubt he's authorized by the National Park Service to do this work, but he seems to know what he's doing. Treefall appears to be increasing. Intense storms, southern pine bark beetles, fungus, and the legacy of past droughts are all impacting the old-growth forest remnants in this wooded ravine. The beetles are relatively common pests in pine forests; their feeding and tunneling activities will eventually girdle an infested tree and kill it.

Cicadas—the iconic soundtrack of summer—are humming loudly in the trees. I descend the trail, discovering more mushrooms in many colors: white, red, and a brown-white swirl. A few tiny flower blossoms are still visible in the forest, despite the August heat.

I cannot hear the river until I am almost to its banks. The reduced weekend releases of water from Buford Dam have resulted, as usual, in extremely low levels. Still, there is enough water to float the bright yellow rafts and colorful kayaks making their way through the shoals and around the sharp bend in the river toward Sandy Point and Diving Rock. As always, the air alongside the river is cool and refreshing, even in summer.

I take photos at my favorite spots, marveling, as I always do, over the mirror images of clouds, trees, and rocks in the clear, still water. On the riverbank, I find a pile of opened freshwater clam shells at the door of a muskrat burrow. A few larger flowers are blooming near the river, including a gorgeous morning glory (*Convolvulaceae*) on its wormy vine: trumpet-like and perfectly white with a fuchsia center. The oyster mushrooms (*Pleurotus ostreatus*) I discovered on a log two weeks ago are gone. In their place are tiny, shriveled remnants.

It's a busy day in the park with people moving quickly along the trail. I revel in my slowness, in the time that I give myself to explore side paths and focus on details. I know that changes will come more quickly as summer ends and cool days alter the tune and timbre of the insects. I want to observe and acknowledge as much as possible. Every time I walk this path, I see something I have never seen before, or see things in any entirely new way: a fresh perspective. Close observation of nature brings many rewards.

At the end of the trail, I sit and watch the ducks in the river with their tails in the air, looking like they are standing on their heads in the water, possibly seeking a tasty morsel or just cooling off. A great blue heron (*Ardea herodias*) stands very near me, perfectly still in the water. Hot and sticky, I walk back along the river and then uphill. My trash bag holds dozens of small pieces of Styrofoam, a few plastic bottles, and a pair of flip-flops.

In many ways, the creation of this national park in the late 1970s helped transform my life at a time when I was searching for a path forward, both personally and professionally. National parks have played similar roles for my sons, helping them mature and fostering their love of nature and adventure while working summer jobs. My older son, Charles, spent a summer in Yellowstone and my younger, Robert, in Yosemite. Their affinity for nature—developed on family trips and at a summer camp in the mountains of North Carolina—deepened during the months they spent in national parks.

Reflecting on my journey to a career as an environmental advocate, I know it had roots in many places: the backyard streams and wooded hill of my childhood home, parents who cared deeply about nature and wildlife, and family vacations on Sanibel Island. Also influential were postcollege hiking and camping adventures with friends, lessons in environmental advocacy learned as a volunteer with the Sierra Club, and an internship with the National Park Service.

On August 15, 1978, President Jimmy Carter signed a bill to create the Chattahoochee River National Recreation Area (CRNRA) as members of a local environmental group called Friends of the River joined him in the Rose Garden ceremony at the White House. I knew several of those individuals—notably Roger Buerki, who encouraged and inspired my early environmental work—and later came to know many others.

These river advocates had fought valiantly and successfully since the early 1970s to protect the Chattahoochee through local land-use battles, state legislation, and finally the designation of a national park on the river. Strategically, they took advantage of opportunities presented during the Nixon administration with its emphasis on "bringing parks to the people."

The same year that the CRNRA was created, I began a two-year master's degree program in city and regional planning at Georgia Tech with a focus on the environment. I had developed a passion for the work and some practical on-the-ground experience as a Sierra Club volunteer. To become an effective advocate, I knew that I needed to learn a great deal more about environmental issues, policy making, and planning at all levels of government.

An internship is a requirement for the master's planning program. Serendipitously, I saw a notice that the National Park Service was seeking summer interns to help develop the first management plan for the CRNRA. I was thrilled to be chosen for the position and still have a copy of the report that two other students and I produced about laws available to protect the river and the park. Only in my dreams could I have foreseen that many years later I would become the director of a new environmental nonprofit, one whose mission is to ensure compliance with these and other environmental laws.

As I worked on the CRNRA's first management plan, I learned that the forty-eight-mile corridor of the CRNRA provides habitat for an amazing variety of living organisms, currently 198 bird species, 59 species of fish, 25 amphibians, more than 41 reptiles, 127 butterflies, and 38 native mammals. Of the nearly 1,000 plant species in the CRNRA, 813 are native to the area. According to the National Park Service, the park "contains the oldest and most extensive protected areas of native vegetation in the Atlanta metropolitan area."

Since the national park was created, many individuals and organizations have worked to help the CRNRA be the best it can be. They include Riverkeeper, Trust for Public Land, Trout Unlimited, and Chattahoochee National Park Conservancy, the official friends group for the park. After my retirement, I served on the Chattahoochee National Park Conservancy's board and chaired it for several years. Among other priority projects, we helped initiate and fund an assessment by professional trail planners for the sixty-five miles of official trails in the national park. This study informed the first-ever comprehensive trails management plan, approved in 2022. The plan is already helping restore the paths that have been loved to death over nearly five decades.

Another initiative called Chattahoochee RiverLands—created by Trust for Public Land and its partners—envisions a 125-mile multimodal path near the river. As a linear network of greenways, water trails, parks, and other destinations, RiverLands has the potential to connect the land units in the CRNRA and enhance the national water trail within the park.

The CRNRA is beloved by the three and a half million people who visit it annually, making the park the nineteenth most visited in the country in 2022—out of 423 national parks. Yet, like every other unit in the national park system, it has a backlog of deferred maintenance projects, which totals about $15 million. Nationally, the National Park Service backlog for its entire park system is an astounding $12 billion.

I will never understand why one of the public's most appreciated federal programs is so poorly supported in congressional budgets. There are advocates, such as the National Parks Conservation Association and others, who fight to protect and enhance our precious national parks and other public lands. People need nature to restore their bodies and minds.

On August 4, 2020, Congress finally passed the Great American Outdoors Act: a landmark conservation bill that had been advocated for decades. By establishing the National Parks and Public Land Restoration Fund, the law provides, at long last, a stable revenue source for federal land stewardship and deferred maintenance projects. It authorizes dedicated funding, up to $1.6 billion annually, for the first five years. The funding comes primarily (and appropriately) from leases to extract oil, gas, and coal from federal lands and waters.

Having enough money to support our national park system is the critical first step. The National Park Service must also have strong leadership and sufficient staff to meet the needs and reasonable expectations of its guests. More than three hundred million people, on average, visit our national parks every year. From an economic perspective, park visitor spending in 2019 contributed more than $40 billion to the U.S. economy. These natural, historic, and cultural landscapes—set aside for everyone for all time—provide enormous value to the American people.

CHAPTER 11

From Apalachicola Adventures to Floating Classrooms

September 1, 2019

Summer is winding down, and I can feel it on the Cabin Creek trail in the way the bugs sound, the stillness in the forest, and the emergence of late summer wildflowers along the river. My grand-dog Randy, a large mixed breed who looks something like a southern black mouth cur, joins me for today's walk. He noses into piles of leaves, scares a fast lizard, sniffs at muskrat burrows, and laps up the clear water in Cabin Creek. It's his second visit to the trail. He shows me many things I otherwise would have missed.

It is a slow walk, talking to people about the park, taking photos, and checking out the forest and river smells. No late summer flowers bloom in the woods. As we approach the river, which is extremely low, I begin to see flashes of color. Tiny purple, lavender, and yellow blossoms appear, along with the fiery red cardinal flower (*Lobelia cardinalis*). A dozen stalks decorate a backwater near the river, where sufficient sunlight encourages their growth. Named for the vivid red color of a Roman Catholic cardinal's robe, these fall wildflowers attract many species of hummingbirds. I also find buttonbush (*Cephalanthus occidentalis*) and joe-pye weed (*Eutrochium purpureum*) with its pale pinkish-purple flowers at the riverbank.

The reflections in the river are as hypnotizing as ever. The light is ever-changing—revealing the sky, clouds, trees, and plants in new perspectives and hues. As the river plays with sunlight to create magic, all of my senses are stimulated. I take a short video of the river flowing through the shoals and around the frozen-wave rocks to share on social media for those homebound this weekend: a peaceful snapshot of rippling water, rustling sycamore leaves, and sunbeams.

Because it's a holiday weekend, the park and its trails are full of people: families with young children and organized groups, including one called Girls Who Hike. The diversity in age and ethnicity represented by the people I meet is encouraging. The young park visitors remind me of the thousands of students who visit Riverkeeper's floating classrooms every year. In these outdoor learning spaces, naturalists and science teachers work to inspire a sense of wonder in the natural world and awe, an essential human emotion.

The waters of the Chattahoochee ultimately flow into Apalachicola Bay and the Gulf of Mexico, more than five hundred miles downstream of the tiny spring in north Georgia's Mark Trail Wilderness that gives birth to the river. From the Georgia-Florida border—where the Chattahoochee meets the Flint River—to the Gulf of Mexico, the waterway is called the Apalachicola River.

By the time the blended freshwater, drained from nearly twenty thousand square miles of land in three states, reaches the bay, the flow is enormous. It is critical to the sustenance of the nationally recognized estuary. The Apalachicola River and Bay comprise one of the most ecologically diverse natural areas in the southern United States. Four barrier islands separate the bay and lagoon system from the gulf.

In the late 1990s, Riverkeeper staff were invited to visit the scientists and advocates working to protect the environment at the downstream end of our river. In addition to enjoying a retreat from the office, our goal was to better understand how the river functions. We wanted to learn how communities along the river—from top to bottom—depend on the ecosystem.

For several years thereafter, our staff regularly traveled to Apalachicola for long weekends to explore the waters of the river and bay by motorboat and kayak. We expanded our knowledge of this magnificent river basin, learning firsthand how dependent the area is on having enough fresh water, delivered seasonally from upstream rivers.

With permission, we camped on one of the barrier islands—Little St. George, also known as Cape St. George—which lies about eight miles offshore of the town of Apalachicola. An uninhabited island owned by the state, which once sported an old lighthouse built in 1852, it is a prime nesting area for endangered loggerhead sea turtles. By the time we experienced the island, storms and beach erosion had left the lighthouse leaning at a precipitous angle. It was vulnerable to wind and water and fell in 2005. Bricks from the toppled structure were moved to nearby, developed St. George Island, where a lighthouse replica was constructed.

On Little St. George, we found shards of thousand-year-old pottery and a small alligator effigy on its bayside beach. We rode all-terrain vehicles on narrow sandy roads through the maritime forest to the gulf beach at night. With lights and noise, we tried to keep raccoons from destroying new turtle nests. We ate raw oysters in the light of bonfires, suffered mosquitoes on summer trips, and took pictures of ourselves pretending to support the leaning lighthouse. We pondered the lives of the more than two dozen lightkeepers and their families who had lived on the island to tend the beacon over its 150-year life.

During one of the long drives back to Atlanta from Apalachicola, we hatched an idea for a new Riverkeeper education program. We would create a floating classroom. Modeling our initiative after similar programs presented by other waterkeepers, we decided to offer students an on-the-water experience by partnering with Elachee Nature Science Center. Located in Gainesville, Georgia, this accredited nature and outdoor learning center was then led by my friend Andrea Timpone.

Because of Elachee's proximity to Lake Lanier—the huge federal reservoir upstream of metro Atlanta—we could easily launch a boat large enough to hold a class of students. Most of the upper half of the Chattahoochee River is too shallow to float such a vessel. We secured funding, designed the pontoon boat for group teaching, and put together a business plan. The objective was to take advantage of the complementary assets offered by Riverkeeper and Elachee. The Lake Lanier Aquatic Learning Center set sail in 2000.

Seven years later, our pontoon boat was replaced with a custom-built forty-foot catamaran: an impressive vessel that continues to ply the waters of Lake Lanier from spring to fall. It provides many students with their first-ever, confidence-building experience on a boat. Celebrating twenty- plus years of operation, this program has brought nearly sixty thousand students on board to learn about the river system that flows from the north Georgia mountains to Apalachicola Bay.

All student trips are subsidized and full scholarships are provided for underserved students, who represent at least a third of the participants every year. A long-standing priority for Riverkeeper is to help disadvantaged youth join this popular program: those who may not have many opportunities for outdoor learning experiences.

For years, Riverkeeper hoped to offer the floating classroom program to Atlanta Public Schools (APS), targeting the system's disadvantaged and underserved youth. An unwritten rule had long prohibited APS students from participating in any on-the-water field trips. Persistence by Riverkeeper's executive director, Juliet Cohen, and other staff paid off. They worked diligently with the APS Superintendent's Office and its legal department to find a way to make the field trips possible.

Agreement was finally reached in 2017. Middle schools in the APS system, including Title I schools with their large percentage of low-income families, are now participating in voyages of discovery on Lake Lanier.

Riverkeeper launched a second floating classroom program on West Point Lake near the city of LaGrange, in 2015, the year after I retired. In a dockside ceremony at which LaGrange mayor Jim Thornton and I broke champagne bottles against her bow, the new boat was christened the *Miss Sally*. It was, and remains, an honor that I count as one of the most meaningful in my career. If a student asks who Miss Sally is, or was, and learns a bit of my riverkeeping story, perhaps she will be inspired to take a similar path in life and fight for our environment. Safeguarding nature helps protect all life, including ourselves.

We sought ways to provide environmental education lessons about the river to students unable to visit our floating classroom. Partnering with the Center for Global Environmental Education at Hamline University, we coproduced an interactive educational tool consisting of a virtual trip down the length of the Chattahoochee-Apalachicola Rivers. It contained science, nature, and history lessons. In 2004 our series of river learning programs won a top award at the Wildscreen Festival, the world's largest festival of nature films.

As the years passed, Riverkeeper developed innovative programs to help people of all ages build relationships with the Chattahoochee and its waters. All Kids Fish is a new program that inspires the next generation of fly anglers and conservationists. Attention is the beginning of devotion, wrote poet Mary Oliver. Devotion leads to action.

A massive leaf from the bigleaf magnolia (*Magnolia macrophylla*), an understory tree, found in late fall in the Cabin Creek ravine, Chattahoochee River National Recreation Area. Photo: Lucie Langford Canfield.

CHAPTER 12

Upside Down in Chattahoochee Whitewater

September 12, 2019

It is not enough to fight for the land; it's even more important to enjoy it. While you can. While it's still here. . . . Explore the forests, climb the mountains, bag the peaks, run the rivers.
—*Edward Abbey*

The sun is bright, shining through the dense, green forest as it climbs into the sky on this early fall day. Walking downhill to the river, I look up to admire the magnificent canopy of bigleaf magnolia leaves (*Magnolia macrophylla*). This unusual deciduous tree with the largest simple leaf of any native plant in North America—at twelve to thirty inches long—is found in the understory of rich, wooded areas in river valleys and ravines in the Southeast. I am in love with these native beauties.

The tall spikes of red cardinal flowers I found on my last walk are now at least three feet above the moist riverbank. In shaded areas, I spot downy lobelia (*Lobelia puberula*), the most common blue-flowered lobelia in the Southeast. The usually one-sided flower spike of the lobelia with its two upper- and three lower-lip lobes comes in a range of colors from light blue to lavender and purple.

Fall is my favorite season to walk along or paddle the Chattahoochee. Some of my best—and most exciting—outdoor adventures have taken place during this spectacular time of year.

Underwater and hanging upside down, I was forced to make my first "wet exit" from my new kayak. Instinctively, I yanked the spray skirt off the boat and pushed up to the river's surface to gasp for air. As my boat, paddle, and I were propelled downstream in the strong current, fellow paddlers moved expertly to my side. They captured my boat, righted it, and dumped out the water. I was safe, but cold and shaken.

Our two-day river trip had begun on a beautiful morning in mid-September, when two dozen paddlers launched a pod of colorful kayaks into the cold water of Sautee Creek in the Nacoochee Valley of White County. We planned to float nineteen miles on the Upper Chattahoochee River Water Trail. At the creek's confluence with the Chattahoochee, I marveled at the transparent water, afloat with early fall leaves. Moss-covered stones on the river bottom were visible in astonishing detail.

Nine miles of paddling took us through one of my favorite sections of the river, its streambanks dense with rhododendron, mountain laurel, fall wildflowers, and towering trees. Then came the Dead Sea, the calm water before Smith Island and its class II rapids. Mention Smith Island to old-timer canoeists and the stories will flow—not just about the whitewater, but also about a gun-toting landowner, now long gone, who threatened paddlers.

At the top of the rapids, Gary Gaines, an expert paddler and Riverkeeper board member, pointed to the line we should take through the whitewater. Single file, with space between our boats, we followed him, hugging the left bank while passing over two rock ledges as the river dropped rapidly, stroking quickly and powerfully to cross to the right bank, then taking a sharp left turn in front of a large rock, before plunging into a deep pool. I was doing fairly well until the boulder loomed before me. I hesitated. In that moment, I missed the left turn and flipped my boat, leading to the clumsy wet exit.

The next day, we again drifted toward turbulent water, paddles motionless. I scanned the rocks in the churning river before me, trying to read the water and find the best route through the rapids. The smooth, clear water under my kayak contrasted sharply with the noisy, agitated cauldron just a hundred feet ahead.

I took a deep breath and followed Gary's red kayak in front of me into the whitewater. I braced my knees against the sides of my boat and dug my paddle deeply into the river. Left, right, left, right. I powered through the waves and away from the rocks. My heart pounding, I shot through the rapids and into calmer waters. Later that day, I made it through more technical rapids (requiring some skill to maneuver) and regained a bit of the confidence I had lost the day before. My paddling mojo was back!

Several years later, on a return trip to this stretch of the Chattahoochee with my older son Charles and a group of river friends, I approached the Smith Island rapids with no small amount of fear and trepidation. Again, I flipped my kayak. I dream about the day I'll deftly make that left turn at the big rock and shoot into the beautiful pool of water below the rapids.

Horse Trough Falls lies several hundred feet below Chattahoochee Gap in the Mark Trail Wilderness of the Chattahoochee-Oconee National Forest. Photo: Tom Wilson.

CHAPTER 13

Water Is Magic, Waterkeepers Are Vigilant

September 22, 2019

> If there is magic on this planet, it is contained in water.
> —*Loren Eiseley*

I love the early evening light as the sun begins to drop behind the forested bluff of the West Palisades on the opposite shore from my path. The river is smooth, flowing quietly downstream around the jagged rocks as night approaches. There are reflections in the water beneath golden clouds. Shadows deepen along the wooded trail.

A few flowers still bloom along the river, catching my eye. Shades of bluish purple in wild ageratum or blue mistflower (*Conoclinium coelestinum*) and downy lobelia. Shades of yellow in goldenrod and black-eyed Susans.

My photos reflect the silver and sepia tones that I see around me in the forest, on the water, and in the sky. However often I walk this trail, it never fails to comfort me. I find peace in my growing intimacy with this place of land and water.

Water is magical. It's not just a liquid that sustains all life, as if that weren't enough—the molecules of oxygen and hydrogen also inspire, energize, and soothe. There's a scientific reason we love flowing, plunging, spraying water, why being around moving water can improve our moods. It's called negative ions: molecules that have gained or lost an electrical charge. They are created in nature when air molecules break apart due to a variety of influences from sunlight to moving water.

The action of falling water and crashing waves (or even a bathroom shower) creates negative ions that bond with smaller air particles. When we breathe in this charged air, the negative ions enter our bloodstream.

They produce biochemical reactions that can relieve stress, boost energy, and reduce depression—affecting serotonin levels. By increasing the flow of oxygen to the brain, the negative ions can also enhance alertness.

It's no wonder that some people decide to spend their lives working to safeguard rivers, creeks, lakes, estuaries, and oceans. When I became a riverkeeper, I joined an eclectic group of folks who live, breathe, and sleep thinking about how to restore their water bodies. They come from all walks of life. Marine biologists, writers, professors, commercial fishers, lawyers, planners, artists, environmentalists, and boat captains.

At some point, each of us made a decision to devote our careers to protecting water, doing whatever it might take to counter the ignorance, apathy, and greed that pollutes and wastes. Despite differences in backgrounds and geography, our passion for clean water makes us a family, at times dysfunctional but still close.

On the Hudson River in New York, American folk music legend Pete Seeger helped spawn the first riverkeeper group with his passion for the waterway he lived on. Outraged by the deteriorating condition of the river in the 1960s, he and his wife built the now-iconic sloop *Clearwater.* The boat served as the initial hub for the revival of the Hudson and has since provided five decades of environmental education programs.

Inspired by Seeger's commitment to that river, the Hudson Riverkeeper was formed by a coalition of commercial and recreational fishermen who met regularly at a local American Legion in the late 1960s. The Hudson was everything to these men. It was where they worked and where they played. It was the centerpiece of their community.

Increasingly, they worried that polluters were taking their river from them and the public with the dumping of sewage, chemicals, oil from railyards, and hot water from power plants. Wetlands, the nurseries for their historic fishery, were being dredged and filled for development. The river was dying, along with their livelihoods. They wanted to do something about it. Vandalism was seriously discussed.

A fisherman and writer for *Sports Illustrated* named Bob Boyle spoke to the crowd at the American Legion. He had discovered two obscure federal laws passed at the turn of the twentieth century; both forbade pollution of U.S. waters and provided penalties and bounties to those who reported it. The fishers resolved that they would use these laws to go after every polluter on the Hudson. They would use the winnings from legal cases to build and launch a boat and start a riverkeeper program.

In 1972 Congress passed the federal Clean Water Act, which gives the public the right to enforce the law by collecting evidence and suing polluters when the government fails to take action. This foundational statute offered additional tools to demand the cleanup of the Hudson and other waterways. The following year, a local commercial fisherman and house painter named John Cronin met Pete Seeger and became involved with the work to save the Hudson, initially as a volunteer.

John was hired as the first full-time paid riverkeeper in the United States in 1983, successfully advocating for the Hudson and its watershed for seventeen years. He took on major polluters such as General Electric, Penn Central, Con Edison, Anaconda, and Exxon. On the Chattahoochee, I worked hard to model my advocacy after John's on the Hudson. His mentorship was an important part of my early riverkeeping years.

The consensus of those involved with the Hudson's cleanup was that a riverkeeper or waterkeeper was needed on every major water body in the country. The protection and enjoyment of a community's natural assets requires the daily vigilance of its citizens. The Waterkeeper Alliance, created in the late 1990s by Robert F. Kennedy Jr. and others, now boasts more than 300 licensed groups around the world in forty-five countries.

One of my favorite photos shows eleven smiling people in front of Maine's Casco Bay. Half the men have bushy beards, and there are just two women—one of them me. We represented the entire waterkeeper movement when this photo was taken in 1995. I remember how excited I was to be in the company of this motley crew of advocates. We had traveled to Maine from California, New Jersey, New York, North Carolina, Pennsylvania, Connecticut, Rhode Island, and Georgia. I was one of the first women to become a waterkeeper, more specifically, a riverkeeper.

We had gathered to talk about expanding the movement and supporting each other. It was an amazing experience, but the expectations implied for my work on the Chattahoochee were daunting. How could I follow in the footsteps of these dedicated and skilled people? I had to figure out how to do what they did so well, but possibly with a southern twist.

As the movement and our annual conferences grew in numbers and in diversity with water advocates from around the world, so did the fun—in addition to useful workshops and inspirational speakers. We networked on the water, in bars, at galas, and in tattoo parlors. Many of the keepers (not me) got the infamous Waterkeeper sturgeon inked on their bodies. We boated with singer Billy Joel on his yacht, *The Redhead*, and listened to Jimmy Buffett at an outdoor gala on Long Island.

On a cocktail cruise on New York City's East River, we gabbed with actor Richard Dean Anderson, who—as MacGyver in the popular television show of the 1980s—righted the wrongs of the world using scientific knowledge and gadgets instead of pistols. We had our pictures taken with former president Bill Clinton and leading climate scientist James Hansen in the Bronx and with Erin Brockovich at a gala in San Francisco.

We listened to brilliant geneticist and environmentalist David Suzuki in Toronto and Mexican president Vincente Fox in La Paz, Baja. Always exhausted, but inspired, we returned to the day-to-day challenges of protecting our home waters.

CHAPTER 14

When the Well Is Dry

October 3, 2019

> Whiskey is for drinking; water is for fighting.
> —*Attributed to Mark Twain*

Ninety-seven degrees in early October! Even so, Randy and I set out, late morning, to walk down Cabin Creek to the river. The severe drought, six weeks and counting with no rain and high temperatures, is evident. Doghobble and mountain laurel leaves hang limp from their branches. Everything looks parched. The trail is dusty, and Cabin Creek is a trickle in some places, though I still find the tiny fish that dart about at the elbow in the creek.

I think I hear a hawk call as other birds sing and Randy plunges down the trail ahead of me, excited to be in the woods. Despite the heat, fall manifests itself in the yellow and brown leaves that have dropped to the floor of the still forest, as well as in the absence of buzzing and clicking cicadas. The air remains cooler at the river. Smells are strong, suggestive of fish, small animals, flower blooms, muddy riverbanks, and decaying plants.

I see dragonflies circling over the whitewater at the bottom of the shoals, swarm-foraging. I wonder if they might be common green darner dragonflies (*Anax junius*) that have migrated from the north. In early spring, first generations of green darners leave southern waters on temperature cues and fly north an average of four hundred miles on their two-inch wings; there, they lay eggs and die. The second generation of green darners hatches in the north and flies south in the fall: an epic, multigenerational migration.

As I expected, the river is very low. I imagine the anxiety on the part of metro Atlanta water supply managers and local utilities. Undoubtedly, they are taking steps to reduce the releases from Buford Dam so that as much water as possible will stay in Lake Lanier. Atlanta's people, businesses, and future growth are their priority, not so much other cities and farms downstream, or sustaining the river ecosystem.

Bright colors decorate the trail: red seeds of American strawberry bush, commonly known as hearts-a-bustin'-with-love (*Euonymus americanus*); goldenrod (*Solidago*); clusters of blue mistflower and lavender downy lobelia. Randy and I slow our pace in the maze-like bamboo forest and watch the river flowing past. I take photos of midday shadows on the thick green stems before it's time to head back.

Tired and damp from the humid air and my exertion, mostly dog management, we follow a couple up the trail along the creek. They stop in the middle of the path and point upslope, exclaiming, "Deer!" We are too far away and can't see them. The deer are gone by the time we reach the spot where the couple stopped, but Randy suddenly behaves like a crazed bloodhound. He knows that something very interesting has crossed our path.

The political and legal conflict among Georgia, Alabama, and Florida over the water in the Chattahoochee and Flint River basins is now in its thirty-third year, with no end in sight. In retirement, I don't miss the interminable meetings and conference calls related to this difficult issue, but I do miss seeing some of the people I came to know.

Most of us hoped to find a path forward: a way to fairly share the water in the river to meet the needs of competing water users and the ecosystem when it doesn't rain—when water levels in the rivers and lakes drop. Whether our decades of work will produce such a positive outcome during the next extreme drought remains to be seen.

More than three decades ago, I attended my first meeting about what has long been called the tristate water wars among Georgia, Alabama, and Florida. It was 1990. That year, Alabama filed a federal lawsuit against Georgia and the U.S. Army Corps of Engineers—the federal agency that operates Buford Dam, making daily decisions on how much of the stored lake water to send through the turbines and downstream to various users. The lawsuit claimed that the Corps of Engineers was holding back what Alabama deemed to be excessive amounts of water in Lake Lanier. The state's lawyers argued that federally required studies had not been conducted, nor had all government approvals been secured.

Georgia's goal—to keep as much water as possible in Lake Lanier on the Chattahoochee—is primarily to be able to supply growth in ever-expanding metro Atlanta. The sprawling region relies on the smallest watershed (land area) in the country serving a major metropolitan area:

a "relative trickle of a waterway," noted an article in the *New York Times*. The Chattahoochee's drainage basin upstream of the city totals just one thousand square miles, or one-eighth of the land area of metro Atlanta.

Second, Georgia is interested in maintaining agricultural production in the lower Flint River basin with sufficient access to groundwater. Droughts are increasing in duration and intensity in this region as well. Much of the groundwater used for irrigation comes from the Flint River's recharge flows into the underground Floridan aquifer.

Enough freshwater inflow to Florida's Apalachicola River and Bay must come from the Chattahoochee, the Flint, or both rivers. The political and geographic boundaries within the Apalachicola-Chattahoochee-Flint (ACF) river basin have a profound bearing on the water conflict.

Alabama's goal is to ensure sufficient river flows during droughts to support its communities and industries that depend on the Chattahoochee, including Farley Nuclear Plant. There is also the state's long-standing political resentment of Atlanta's control of water flowing downstream from Georgia into Alabama. During the 1990s and early 2000s, both states blasted barbed editorial cartoons back and forth across the Chattahoochee.

Florida got involved in the water fight in late 1990 by filing a legal action against Georgia and the Corps of Engineers. The downstream state was worried about the impacts of increasing upstream water consumption on the viability of its seafood industry in Apalachicola Bay during droughts. The bay requires sufficient freshwater inflow to support oysters, shrimp, and other species. Historically, the Apalachicola River, fed by the Chattahoochee and Flint Rivers, has delivered more water into the Gulf of Mexico than any other river except the Mississippi.

More than thirty years later, the legal battles, political conflict, and droughts continue. Some questions have been answered; others remain. Georgia won a 2021 case in which the U.S. Supreme Court unanimously dismissed a water rights case that Florida had brought against Georgia eight years earlier. (Multiple legal actions are being pursued as the parties employ various strategies.)

Florida's loss was due, in no small part, to its flawed legal strategy and failure to present sound, scientific support for its arguments. Based on the evidence presented, the court did not agree that harm to the state's oyster population—dependent on a delicate balance between freshwater and saltwater—was the result of Georgia's upstream water use.

In its decision, the court reminded Georgia of the state's obligation to make reasonable use of the rivers in the ACF river basin "to help conserve that increasingly scarce resource." Water conservation programs conducted by local and state government agencies in Georgia were deemed legally reasonable. This means that the water efficiency laws, policies, and other tools must remain in place. Importantly, the court also acknowledged the role of climate change and its effects on rivers.

To summarize: Georgians have a responsibility to conserve water, according to the U.S. Supreme Court. For the state to keep growing, it must implement new ways to save water in cities, industries, and farms. Riverkeeper and others believe that, at the end of the day, it may not be legal challenges but the challenges of climate change that will drive future water decisions.

Although it cannot be rehearsed quickly, the history of the longest-running interstate water dispute in the eastern United States is worth reviewing. Conflicts like ours in the ACF basin can lead to environmental harm and inequitable outcomes, resulting in water-use haves and have-nots. These natural resource battles are increasing rapidly worldwide as the earth's population soars and climate change accelerates. The role of public interest nonprofits in the equity and environmental aspects of water sharing agreements cannot be overstated.

In the 1940s and 1950s, Congress passed legislation authorizing the construction of four large dams on the mainstem of the Chattahoochee River. Buford Dam, which created Lake Lanier when it was completed in 1957, is the farthest upstream reservoir. Given the area's mountainous topography, Lanier is also the deepest with the greatest water storage capacity.

Congress authorized Buford Dam to be managed by the Corps of Engineers for power generation, flood control, and navigation. Water in the lake would be released as needed to help maintain a nine-foot-deep river channel hundreds of miles downstream for commercial barges. Barge traffic from the gulf upstream to Columbus, Georgia, was much greater in the mid-twentieth century than it is today. Columbus lies at Georgia's Fall Line, the Mesozoic-era shoreline of the Atlantic Ocean, where rivers now plunge from basically the same elevation. Navigation upstream is not viable without massive river engineering.

At the time, water supply for metro Atlanta was considered an "additional benefit" of building Buford Dam and Lake Lanier, but it was not a stated, congressionally designated purpose.

When Congress authorized the construction of Buford Dam in 1946, then–Atlanta mayor William Hartsfield refused to help pay for the dam fifty miles upstream of his city. He said, "The benefit [of the Lake Lanier project] is only incidental and in case of a prolonged drought. The city of Atlanta has many sources of potential water supply in north Georgia. Certainly, a city which is only one hundred miles below one of the greatest rainfall areas in the nation will never find itself in the position of a city like Los Angeles." Famous last words.

Hartsfield's comments were cited more than sixty years later, in 2009, by U.S. District Court Judge Paul Magnuson, who ruled that the metro Atlanta region was not legally authorized to use the lake for water supply. He gave the states three years to find a way to fairly allocate water during droughts. Called a draconian action even by the judge, the order got the states' attention. Two years later, Magnuson's order was overturned by the Eleventh Circuit Court of Appeals.

Except during extreme, multiyear droughts, the ACF river basin has enough water to supply reasonable demands placed on it by municipalities, industries, and farmers. Whether the ecosystems in the ACF basin can be sustained under various river management scenarios, such as how federal dams on the Chattahoochee are operated and whether water pumped from the river is returned, remains uncertain. Despite the efforts of environmentalists and scientists, the ecological aspect of the conflict has not (yet) received enough attention from decision makers.

As time passed, metro Atlanta began to experience more frequent droughts: three severe droughts in the 1980s, a lengthy drought from 1998 to 2003, and an exceptional drought from late 2006 to early 2009, when Lake Lanier plummeted to a record nineteen feet below its normal level. Another severe drought occurred from 2012 to 2014, followed by shorter flash droughts in 2016 and 2019. While long dry spells have happened for thousands of years in the Southeast, they are coming more frequently and with more severity. Global heating will continue and exacerbate this trend.

There is also evidence that the 1960s, when engineers planned the metro region's water supply infrastructure, was an abnormally wet climatic period. They did not expect the recurring, deeper drought periods that we are now seeing and anticipating. Compounding these problems is the fact that soils are drying out. The inflow to the river system from groundwater is diminishing; this tracks with altered rainfall patterns that seem to be due largely to climate change.

In the late 1990s, the three states decided to suspend their legal actions to seek mutual agreement on how to divvy up the water in the ACF basin among competing interests during droughts. The hope was for a negotiated compact: a formal, legislatively enacted agreement. It could fairly and equitably divide the water among the three states and their competing demands during low flow periods.

Conservationists in all three states believe the ACF basin should be managed for human benefit in a way that also sustains the ecosystem, protects water quality, and supports recreational uses. The three waterkeeper groups in the basin are striving to achieve this goal. I worked closely with Dan Tonsmeire on the Apalachicola River and Gordon Rogers on the Flint River, both colleagues and friends. Our organizations' collective commitment to resolving the water conflict fairly and equitably continues today.

In late 1996 those of us paying attention to the interstate water conflict began to hear rumors. Negotiators in the three states were working behind the scenes to draft bills for passage by their state legislatures and ultimately the U.S. Congress. That legislation would create an ACF compact to serve as a general framework to guide collaborative efforts with specifics to come later. Those specifics would be based on a major comprehensive study that would answer questions about existing water use and availability. But why the secrecy?

The speculation, later confirmed, was that compact legislation was being drafted by the states in such a way that it would allow them to make decisions about interstate waters without being guided (or constrained, some claimed) by federal environmental laws passed in the 1970s. In other words, state decisions could supersede these laws. Federal environmental and wildlife agencies were opposed to such a maneuver, as were environmental groups.

As a member of then-congressman Newt Gingrich's environmental advisory committee, I had repeatedly expressed my concerns about the lack of transparency in the legislative drafting to one of his aides. I suggested that the compacts be tabled until the bills were evaluated and revised. She conveyed my concerns to Gingrich, who was the House Speaker at the time. He decided to call a meeting of officials, including Georgia's attorney general and representatives of ten federal agencies, to review the matter.

Riverkeeper's first general counsel, David Moore, joined me at the meeting, which took place in the Speaker's office in north Atlanta. It started in the morning on a Saturday in early January 1997, just a few days before Georgia's legislature was to convene. Gingrich told the assembled group that any attempt to resolve the water conflict with a plan that ignored the seminal federal environmental laws was a nonstarter. He said attempting to circumscribe federal law would delay, if not prevent, any congressional ratification. With those words, Gingrich leveled the playing field.

Gingrich also spoke at length about the need for adequate monitoring of the entire river system "so school children can learn how the river works and who uses it." He was passionate about his home waters—the Chattahoochee River.

I was surprised to hear such sentiments from Gingrich, who was then in the middle of his slash-and-burn term as House Speaker. Despite having been called an outspoken science booster, just a few years earlier, he had played a key role in dismantling the nonpartisan U.S. Office of Technology Assessment. The agency had been established to provide Congress with "competent, nonbiased information." As the years have passed, Gingrich's environmental interests seem to have been replaced with other political ambitions.

At 2:30 a.m., we were assured the federal compact legislation would clarify environmental concerns. The outcome was worth our exhaustion and hunger; dinner had been potato chips and pretzels. It was also worth the heated discussions and multiple phone calls and faxes to state capitals and high officials in Washington. I still have the group photo taken in the wee hours and signed by Gingrich to commemorate the event. The need to protect water quality, ecology, and biodiversity pursuant to environmental laws would be included in the federal legislation. More robust public participation in the water allocation process would be required.

Within months, the ACF compact legislation passed in all three states and was ratified by the U.S. Congress. The importance of considering environmental impacts in water allocation decisions had finally become a meaningful factor. Gingrich's intervention was essential in this positive outcome, setting a precedent for future water negotiations.

Six years later—after the expenditure of $20 million on a comprehensive study—the ACF compact imploded in 2003. Consensus could not be reached among the parties. Disagreements centered around minimum flow requirements at key locations along the rivers: how low the rivers would be allowed to drop at these locations during droughts through water hoarding in upstream reservoirs. Agreement could not be reached on the operation of federal dams during droughts; water consumption caps, if any, for metro Atlanta; and agricultural water use in the Flint basin.

Bad faith on the part of Georgia, alleged by the other two states, and a general lack of transparency also helped kill the compact. It was back to the courts and putting still more taxpayer dollars in lawyers' pockets.

Twenty years have now passed since the ACF compact negotiations failed. Tens of millions of dollars have been spent on high-priced lawyers who have evidenced little interest in resolving the water war equitably among the parties. Their billable hours help keep the fight going. While these lawyers parried and jousted in front of judges, metro Atlanta continued to grow: in the decade from 2010 to 2020, it was the fourth-fastest-growing metropolitan statistical area in the nation.

Severe droughts have continued to pit competing water users against each other, as each period of heavy rainfall suppressed memories of drier times. Inevitably, the behavior of state leaders has seesawed along with the weather. From denial of the water crisis and global heating to improvements in managing limited supplies, and back to denial.

Sadly, too many of these leaders still cast the water conflict as a battle between millions of people in Atlanta and oysters in Apalachicola Bay. As writer Upton Sinclair said: "It is difficult to get a man to understand something, when his salary depends on his not understanding it."

In 2010 an important water conservation measure, the Georgia Water Stewardship Act, passed the state legislature. While conservation progress has been made, Riverkeeper and others have identified more reductions in metro Atlanta's water use that can still be achieved: expedited changes to plumbing codes, aggressive appliance replacement, and fully funded rebate programs, to name a few, all easy initiatives that could lessen stress on rivers and people during droughts. These recommendations have been mostly ignored.

In 2012 the oyster industry in Apalachicola Bay collapsed because of a lack of fresh water from upstream rivers, overharvesting, and other factors. The U.S. Supreme Court and two successive "special masters," charged by the court with overseeing aspects of the Florida-Georgia litigation, became directly involved in the water fight in the following years.

In 2020 Florida closed the bay's iconic oyster fishery for five years to try and save it, allowing its wild oyster reefs time to regenerate. The multimillion-dollar industry once provided 10 percent of the nation's supply and livelihoods for generations of tongers, who use long-handled tongs to harvest oysters from the bay.

Some local governments in metro Atlanta are leading the way with conservation programs to detect and repair leaks, retrofit old-fashioned plumbing fixtures, and reduce outdoor watering. Riverkeeper staff have worked diligently over the years, using our "Tapped Out" presentation and "Filling the Water Gap" reports, to help the public and decision makers understand the many benefits of conserving water, which also saves energy.

It takes a massive amount of energy to pump, heat, treat, and move water to and from people and businesses. Less water consumption means less energy consumption and a reduction in the greenhouse gas emissions that are fueling climate change.

Metro Atlanta has reason to celebrate the fact that it uses less water today, despite population growth. That said, much more can and must be done. Disappointingly, the state continues to approve new, unnecessary withdrawals from the Chattahoochee, along with volume increases for existing water providers. More troubling, water conservation plans for the metro region proposed in 2022 offer few meaningful actions. While needed changes to the plumbing code have been put forward, other conservation commitments have been reduced.

Amid the years of political and legal deadlock, a self-selected group called ACF Stakeholders has worked tirelessly to resolve the water conflict outside the courts. Representing fourteen water-use sectors—from agriculture, drinking water, and industry to recreation, navigation, and ecology—the ACF Stakeholders has met hundreds of times since 2009. Its mission is to understand its members' water needs and find equitable methods of sharing limited water supplies during droughts.

From the earliest discussions and facilitated workshops, it became clear that policy controversies and water management decisions were being driven much more by differences in values and politics than by technical issues.

The ACF Stakeholders has received significant private funding, primarily raised by former board member and retired manufacturing executive Brad Currey. These funds supported studies, analysis, and computer models developed by university scientists. A highly respected businessman and civic leader in Atlanta, Currey provided essential leadership that kept the stakeholder group going over the years.

In 2015 the fifty-six-member ACF Stakeholders board, including Riverkeeper, approved a sustainable water management plan by consensus. Its recommendations were presented to state officials. The thoroughly negotiated and detailed document offers an element of real hope that all reasonable water needs can be met during extreme droughts. Thus far, the plan has been largely ignored by state and federal officials, at least in their public statements and actions.

Meanwhile, we wait for the next drought, when we will think of Benjamin Franklin and his famous words written nearly three centuries ago in *Poor Richard's Almanac*: "When the well's dry, we know the worth of water."

This beautiful brown trout (*Salmo trutta*) was caught in the Chattahoochee River National Recreation Area below McGinnis Ferry. Photo: Justin Dobson.

CHAPTER 15

Negotiating on Behalf of Fish and Clean Water

October 23, 2019

No issue can be negotiated unless you first have the clout
to compel negotiation.
—*Saul Alinsky*

In celebration of his seventy-second birthday, my partner, Neill Herring, and I decide to walk the Cabin Creek trail. It is a beautiful, mild October day, the first walk at the river I've taken since completing a tree identification course at the John C. Campbell Folk School.

Examining leaves, nuts, fruits, acorns, bark, and trunks, we identify twenty tree species in the Cabin Creek ravine. We find black walnut (*Juglans nigra*), tulip poplar (*Liriodendron tulipifera*), sourwood (*Oxydendrum arboreum*), northern red oak (*Quercus rubra*), white oak (*Quercus alba*), chestnut oak (*Quercus montana*), American sycamore or planetree (*Platanus occidentalis*), American basswood (*Tilia americana*), river birch (*Betula nigra*), and bigleaf magnolia (*Magnolia macrophylla*). And we find southern magnolia (*Magnolia grandiflora*), American beech (*Fagus grandifolia*), hickory (*Carya*), red maple (*Acer rubrum*), silver maple (*Acer saccharinum*), willow oak (*Quercus phellos*), American holly (*Ilex opaca*), flowering dogwood (*Cornus florida*), and loblolly and short-leaf pines (*Pinus*). Such astonishing diversity!

Bigleaf magnolia leaves litter the forest floor and I show Neill how I have learned to identify them by the rounded, B-shaped lobes at the base of their leaves. They differ from the V-shaped leaf bases of the umbrella magnolia (*Magnolia tripetala*), a native also prevalent in southern woods.

At the edge of the river, water-loving American sycamores offer a striking presence without their leaves. Where the grayish-brown bark has peeled away in the upper portions of the tall trees, ghostly white branches and trunks stand in stark contrast against the bright blue sky. The brittle bark of the sycamore is unable to accommodate the fast growth of its trunk and branches; it cracks and exfoliates in irregular pieces, resulting in camouflage patterns.

Spiky-looking seed balls, slightly smaller than a ping-pong ball and surprisingly soft to the touch when mature, hang from sycamore branches on tough stems—hence the common name buttonball tree. In the spring, the fruit clusters fall to the ground or into nearby waters. With the help of the wind, hundreds of small seeds within them are dispersed; fine, fluffy hairs attached to the railroad-spike-shaped seeds send them skyward.

People often disparage the massive size and messiness of sycamore trees—the bark, large leaves, and balls that clutter the ground beneath them—and discourage their planting in landscaped areas. I would welcome any amount of clutter to live near such a magnificent tree. I've long been attracted to the broad shape and size of the sturdy sycamore leaves. Until my attentive rambles at the river, I had never noticed the hundreds of small balls on each tree. From late fall to spring, they swing in the wind: dotted silhouettes against the winter sky.

⁓

Neill notices that several old trails leading downhill to the river appear to have once been roads. One is near the stone ruins at the confluence of Cabin Creek and the river. A second leads upslope into the woods near the bamboo forest. Park ranger Jerry Hightower tells me that, in the mid-twentieth century, picnickers drove down to the river for scenic views at the cabin.

Continuing their journeys, the sightseers would drive upstream along the river to the second dirt road, where their cars could head back uphill in a scenic loop. Because cars in those days had limited power to make it back up the steep hill, an enterprising person (or persons) installed a substantial gasoline engine and winch to haul them up to more level ground. On an earlier walk, I had climbed up the hill and found the equipment remains; they had puzzled me at the time.

Walking back along the river trail, we meet several young people wearing Student Conservation Association shirts. They tell us that they'll be working in the national park for a month. The organization was created in the 1950s to build the next generation of conservation leaders through service opportunities, outdoor skills, and leadership training.

Suddenly, a hiker on the trail shouts: "Look!" We all turn our attention to the middle of the Chattahoochee. A North American river otter (*Lontra canadensis*) cavorts in the fast-moving water. Otters are known for their playfulness and this one is no exception, as she (or he) puts on quite a show.

Does she know or care that we are watching her? The otter dives into the water and comes up a short distance downstream with what appears to be a fish in her mouth, possibly a trout. Underwater again, and then she emerges upstream—splashing and flipping her long body, propelling herself with her powerful tail, even leaping several feet into the air. It is a joyful performance that is repeated to our great pleasure and clearly hers.

In a moment of startling clarity, I realize that the Chattahoochee—this life-sustaining flow of fresh water—truly belongs to the otter and her kin, to the fish that may be her dinner, and to all the wildlife who depend on the river. They and their ancestors have lived in and near it for thousands of years, thriving on its bounty sustainably without harming its many gifts for others. As natural historian David Attenborough has noted, humans have a duty to remember that we are "intruders" and "latecomers" to the planet.

A passage from "The Marginal World" in Rachel Carson's 1955 book *The Edge of the Sea* comes to mind. After observing a ghost crab one evening, she wrote:

> *Once, exploring the night beach, I surprised a small ghost crab in the searching beam of my torch. He was lying in a pit he had dug just above the surf, as though watching the sea, and waiting. The blackness of the night possessed water, air, and beach. It was the darkness of an older world, before Man. There was no sound, but the all-enveloping, primeval sounds of wind blowing over water and sand, and of waves crashing on the beach. There was no other visible life— just one small crab near the sea. I have seen hundreds of ghost crabs in other settings, but suddenly I was filled with the odd sensation that for the first time I knew the creature in its own world—that I understood, as never before, the essence of its being. In that moment, time was suspended; the world to which I belonged did not exist and I might have been an onlooker from outer space. The little crab alone with the sea became a symbol that stood for life itself—for the delicate, destructible, yet incredibly vital, force that somehow holds its place amid the harsh realities of the inorganic world.*

Nature doesn't belong to humans. We belong to the earth and the natural systems that sustain all species. We need nature, but it doesn't need us. We are an integral part of the evolution of all life on this planet. Will we ever start behaving in a way that reflects this fundamental truth?

Every day, consequential decisions are made about nature: the air, land, water, plants, and wildlife upon which we all depend. In this country, environmental decisions are typically made by elected and appointed officials, with public input when allowed.

In the 2000s, I served as an appointed official with the Georgia Board of Natural Resources, whose mission is "to sustain, enhance, protect, and conserve Georgia's natural, historic, and cultural resources for present and future generations, while recognizing the importance of promoting the development of commerce and industry that utilize sound environmental practices." My years on this board resulted in more than a few difficult debates and negotiations on behalf of nature.

Appointed by Governor Roy Barnes, a Democrat, and reappointed by Governor Sonny Perdue, a Republican, I served for seven and a half years as a member of the Georgia Board of Natural Resources.

In the summer of 1999, I unexpectedly received a call from Barnes's chief of staff, who asked if I would serve on the board. The governor had campaigned on a promise to diversify the decision-making body, long dominated by monied interests and campaign donors, almost exclusively male and white. As I was a woman and an environmentalist, Barnes apparently hoped I would help bring his promised diversity.

I told his chief of staff that I would be honored to serve but that I would continue my full-time work as an environmental advocate with Riverkeeper—the organization's legal actions and policy positions were at times adverse to the State. He said that they had checked with the state attorney general's office. There was no problem with my continued advocacy.

Many years later, I learned that Barnes had decided to offer me the board position based, at least in part, on the positive recommendation of his friend Bob Matthews, the head of one of the largest road-building firms in the state. In 1995 dirty stormwater and material from an asphalt processing facility owned by C. W. Matthews Contracting Co. was polluting the river in Cobb County. Riverkeeper had threatened to sue the company.

A savvy businessman who clearly understood risk management, Matthews agreed to work with us to remedy the problem. The company removed a one-hundred-ton stockpile of used asphalt from the edge of the river, built a stormwater detention pond to manage storm runoff, and stabilized the riverbank at a cost of about $350,000. It also helped us remove a large trash dump on public land adjacent to their facility by contributing equipment, manpower, and proper disposal of the trash.

Riverkeeper lauded these efforts in the media and worked with the U.S. EPA to give the company a community partnership award. A situation that could have devolved into a bitter, lengthy dispute was resolved cooperatively, always our preference.

Building on this early success, Riverkeeper has, to date, investigated more than six hundred additional industrial sites in the Chattahoochee watershed and secured compliance with clean water laws at 160 of them through education, negotiations, and legal actions.

Within a few weeks of the swearing-in ceremony, Governor Barnes contacted me and former lieutenant governor Pierre Howard, a conservationist who Barnes had also appointed to the board. The governor wanted to address the controversy over north Georgia's trout streams: the southernmost extent of such streams in the eastern United States.

Barnes asked us to meet with two representatives from Georgia's mountain region. Our task was to come to an agreement regarding an environmental regulation affecting trout streams and adjacent landowners. Ten years earlier, a new state law had mandated protections for the natural, vegetative buffers along all state waters: a twenty-five-foot setback buffer along warmwater streams and a much larger, one-hundred-foot buffer along the state's high-quality coldwater trout streams in north Georgia.

Two of the biggest threats to Georgia's trout fisheries are eroded soil and warm water in streams where shoreline trees and plants have been removed. With new construction near waterways escalating in the mountains and with pressure from anglers and conservationists to enforce the buffer law, many property owners were confused and unhappy; some were just plain mad.

The negotiation process, which took place over three months and resulted in a settlement signed in late 1999, was one of the toughest that I experienced in my riverkeeping years. Barnes had made it clear to us that he was going to push both sides as much as necessary to resolve the matter. He certainly had the clout to do so. I was negotiating on behalf of the public and the environmental community—a fact that made the process highly stressful.

At the outset, many of my environmental colleagues felt that we shouldn't give an inch on the width of the one-hundred-foot buffer on trout streams, doubting we'd ever get that much protection again. I explained that, unfortunately, with no legal guidance to instruct the Georgia Environmental Protection Division on how it should issue permits and variances for proposed development in buffer areas, the law was little more than notional.

Among other problems, there wasn't a definition of a "buffer" anywhere in the law, and the EPD director, Harold Reheis at the time, routinely gave variances for builders to encroach in the stream setback. There was simply no formal process and no reliable data upon which to evaluate the impacts of land-disturbing activities taking place adjacent to trout streams.

Ultimately, Pierre and I agreed to reduce the width of buffers along coldwater trout streams in north Georgia from one hundred feet to fifty feet. It was an extremely difficult compromise. In return, we gained the state's commitment to create a functional permit program that provided clear buffer definitions, protection for headwater springs, specific criteria for the issuance of variances, and enforcement measures and closed a development loophole in forestry exemptions. The agreement also included substantial funding for multiyear studies by the University of Georgia.

UGA's Institute of Ecology would assess the impacts of natural buffers of varying widths on water quality and trout habitat for the first time in Georgia, and the Vinson Institute of Government would evaluate associated state policies. Governor Barnes promised that, in his second term, he would review these studies and use them as the basis for any needed amendments to the trout stream buffer law. Our compromise was codified by amendments to Georgia's erosion control law, which passed in the

2000 legislative session. They had the support, if not enthusiasm, of most of the stakeholders.

Two years later, Barnes lost his reelection campaign in an upset. His promised reconsideration of the state's policy on trout stream buffer protection—based on the scientific and policy studies—never occurred.

The authors of the trout buffer studies were asked to present their findings to a state legislative committee. Eight UGA researchers had worked at forty stream sites over three years to produce an extensive data set, the first study to quantify the consequences of narrower stream buffers on water quality and aquatic habitat. The study's conclusion: the reduction in buffer width from one hundred feet to fifty feet would harm trout streams.

One of the authors, Judy Meyer, a stream ecologist with the Institute of Ecology, served on the Riverkeeper board at the time. When she and her colleagues made their presentation to the legislative committee, Senator Chip Pearson—a developer from north Georgia and a Republican notorious for his anti-environmental perspective—declared that the study should be discarded. It was "biased," he said, because of Meyer's advisory role with our organization.

While we were disappointed that the stream buffer study has not (yet) been used to support additional protections for trout streams, we celebrated. Our hard-fought negotiations had resulted in a better, though far from perfect, state decision-making process. No longer could EPD simply rubber-stamp every request to bulldoze the native vegetation and trees along Georgia's waterways.

Saprotrophic mushrooms (*Mycena*) are decomposers that break down dead tissue from wood, plants, and animals. Photo: Alan Cressler.

CHAPTER 16

Pollution Detectives

October 29, 2019

All flourishing is mutual.
—*Robin Wall Kimmerer*

I meet Cynthia Patterson at the Indian Trail parking area on another stunning fall day to walk down Cabin Creek. As is our habit, we pick up man-made debris, including "micro-trash": those tiny bits of human manufacture that litter the ground everywhere. At the trailhead, we're welcomed by a pumpkin carved with an anime design.

Wet leaves cover the ground, blown down from a recent storm. Notable along the trail are the bright yellow leaves from tulip poplars; the huge magnolia leaves have mostly landed with their silvery bottoms facing up, making oblong patterns across the forest floor. Fat brown acorns, the fruit of the oak trees that grow in the creek ravine, cover the ground. Dozens of forest species rely on these nutrient-rich nuts, which help sustain them through the winter.

Since I was a child, I have loved the smooth feel of acorns and the scaly, woody cups that hold them: perfect fairy bowls or hats for elves. As an adult, I have learned that white oak acorn cups have knobby, warty scales, while red oak acorns have flat, pointed scales. Impressively, oak trees in North America annually produce more nuts than all other nut trees together, wild and cultivated.

Halfway down the creek trail, we find a large mushroom that has emerged from the leaf litter since my last visit: an old mushroom of the genus *Amanita*, which includes six hundred species. I kneel and photograph it from underneath to capture the papery gills that produce its spores.

The mushroom is the visible fruiting body of a fungus, an underground organism made up of incredibly tiny, branching threads (hyphae). Extending throughout the soil, the hyphae break down mineral nutrients for their own needs while also making them available to plants. In undisturbed soils, mycelium (fungus-root) networks, made up of bundles of hyphae, connect the roots of individual plants and trees to one another in symbiotic relationships. They circulate nutrients, water, minerals, and even chemical signals in exchange for energy, in the form of carbohydrates generated by photosynthesis. Creating mycorrhizal relationships, some fungi sheath or encase the plant roots, while others tap directly into root cells.

Fungi are heterotrophs. Like humans, they can't produce their own food, so they must obtain sugars from their surroundings. Plants and trees ably fill this role. Fungi are the drivers in this subterranean circulatory system that weaves a "web of reciprocity": an arrangement of mutual aid among trees, plants, and themselves. Scientists have not determined yet whether plants learned to farm fungi or fungi learned to farm plants.

While trees often compete for sun and position in the forest, studies have found that they can also assist each other underground by way of this fungal network. In *The Hidden Life of Trees*, German forester Peter Wohlleben writes: "Whichever tree has an abundance of sugar hands some over; whoever is running short gets help. Fungi are involved. Their enormous networks act as redistribution mechanisms. . . . When trees grow together, nutrients and water can be optimally divided among them all."

Written to inform and appeal to a wide audience, Wohlleben's popular book has been described as over-the-top for using language that anthropomorphizes trees. Yet in its basic premise, *Hidden Life* tracks the groundbreaking work of Suzanne Simard, the insightful and determined forest ecologist who, in the late 1990s, documented mutualistic relationships among forest trees and plants in natural settings. Simard calls these relationships the woodwide web of communication and resource sharing.

Amazingly, hundreds of miles of the mycelium networks can be found under a single human footprint in the forest, connecting plants with resources and sending chemical signals. Much of the world is stitched together by this ecologically connected tissue. According to biologist and author Merlin Sheldrake, fungi are "brokers of entanglement able to mediate the interactions between plants, according to their own fungal needs."

Some five hundred million years ago, fungi likely facilitated the movement of green algae from the ocean onto land, supporting the subsequent evolution and colonization of plants. Sheldrake writes, "This ancient association gave rise to all recognizable life on land, the future of which depends on the continued ability of plants and fungi to form healthy relationships." These fungal networks make up between a third and half of the living mass of soils. They also serve as a major global carbon sink and provide the base of food webs that support nearly all living systems on earth.

At the river, the bright sun is shining on a green anole lizard (*Anolis carolinensis*), perched motionless on the stem of a shrub. We admire its long pointed head and turquoise-rimmed eyes before it scampers up the stem, then jumps into the underbrush and disappears. Soapwort gentians (*Gentiana saponaria*), with their beautiful deep-purple blooms, grow near the water, providing rich fall color.

I continue to think about the abundance of life underground and the interconnections that are taking place among species, reminded that all flourishing (and withering) is mutual. As we expand our knowledge of these out-of-sight organisms and their role in sustaining life above ground, we must find ways to safeguard them and ourselves.

The underground natural world is fascinating. So much life and so many organisms and natural resources that are critical to the existence of humans and all life forms can be found there—unseen, underappreciated, and often unknown altogether. It is also a place where man-made products such as gasoline, oil, and chemicals can seep over years and decades. These products harm underground organisms and will eventually pollute nearby waterways and drinking water wells.

When gravity sewer lines are not regularly maintained and repaired, cracks and breaks in lines that follow streams down gradient can leak waste into groundwater and subsequently nearby streams. Breaches in landfills and malfunctioning septic systems can also threaten rivers from their subterranean sources. Out of sight, out of mind, until it's not.

One of the first calls to Riverkeeper's Citizen Hotline—a few months after the Atlanta office opened—came from an individual reporting gasoline leaks into the river near Helen, a small town in north Georgia. This section of the river has barely a foot of water in it much of the year and, in warmer weather, is filled with tubers and rafters. I remember the caller's vivid description of the strong gasoline smells at the riverbank behind his barbecue restaurant. He said that flames would erupt when he dropped a burning match on the ground.

Investigating the matter, we learned from the Georgia Environmental Protection Division that gasoline had been seeping into the ground next to the restaurant for at least a decade. The sources were failing underground storage tanks at an abandoned gas station on the banks of the river. Rafters and property owners had reported noxious fumes, blackened rocks and leaves, and gasoline visibly seeping from half a dozen spots into the river. Efforts by the state to find and stop the pollution were going slowly—much too slowly.

In phone calls, meetings, and correspondence, we urged the state to take immediate action and make the issue a top priority. Our persistence paid off. A determination was made within a few months that the investigation and subsequent cleanup met the criteria for government funding. The state finally moved quickly to take control of the situation. More than five thousand gallons of gasoline and seven hundred thousand gallons of contaminated groundwater were removed from the site during the state-managed three-year cleanup.

Why would anyone allow underground tanks filled with gasoline to be placed immediately adjacent to a waterway, given the possibility of human error and natural disaster? Over the years, we have repeatedly asked ourselves this question. Regrettably, most of these threatening land uses have been approved by local or state officials.

With an average of two hundred calls per year from concerned individuals to the Riverkeeper Citizen Hotline, staff are constantly busy working to resolve reported problems. As often as possible, they teach callers how to take action themselves. Keeping watch over a community's waterways requires a battalion of informed citizens. During my years with Riverkeeper, it was not unusual for someone to initiate their call by saying, "I have contacted the Georgia EPD and the U.S. EPA, but they can't help me. They said I should call you."

We had our share of callers who exaggerated problems. Others were obviously trying to get their neighbors in trouble, or perhaps had some other agenda. We learned to detect these sham complaints before committing our limited staff to such non-problems. In our first twenty-five years, Riverkeeper responded to calls from more than five thousand individuals. The people and stories behind these calls and emails ranged from alarming and puzzling to amusing, inspirational, and downright impressive.

In the early 2000s, a federal scientist called the hotline to report a particularly nasty situation not far from our office in Atlanta. While monitoring city streams, he had found masses of bacteria strands—a sign of chronic pollution—in a tributary to Proctor Creek. Curiously, he had also found dozens of orange peels floating among the fecal matter. Unable to get the Georgia EPD to respond, the scientist turned to Riverkeeper.

I remember walking down the rocky embankment and through a large culvert to examine the creek. I looked upstream. The imposing edifice of the Fulton County Jail—an overburdened facility whose infrastructure had been failing for years—dominated the landscape.

I called Bert Langley at EPD. After confirming the creek's septic condition (infected with bacteria), Langley's emergency team cordoned off the creek and investigated. They learned that broken toilets and sewer pipes regularly overflowed at the jail, sending the waste downstream. The prisoners were in the habit of throwing their orange peels into toilets, along with the usual material. The county was forced to repair its collapsing infrastructure.

Landowners adjacent to Nancy Creek watched in horror one summer as dead fish floated past their homes in north Atlanta. Several citizens called Riverkeeper, collected dead fish, and spoke with the media. The entire eighteen-mile length of this Chattahoochee tributary had been sterilized by highly chlorinated water. At least fifteen thousand fish and other creatures died in the toxic, drought-stressed waters. Informed citizens' immediate action and evidence helped state officials trace the sources: a chlorine spill from a DeKalb County drinking water plant and the draining of several swimming pools.

A retired schoolteacher named Mildred Burdette called us about muddy water flowing off construction sites and into streams in Hogansville. Developers were simply ignoring the law in the small town, until we got involved. We also worked with Burdette to stop a development company from securing permits to build 2,500 homes on a one-thousand-acre tract of land near a local reservoir that at the time served as the town's only drinking water supply. Concerns about anticipated storm runoff and erosion into the reservoir, as well as inadequate infrastructure to serve the development, slowed the project down. It was never completed.

A. J. James reported that construction related to the expansion of a state detention facility was degrading her subdivision. The Georgia Department of Corrections (DOC) and its contractors were allowing muddy stormwater to flow into her community's lakes and wetlands in south Fulton County. When it became clear that DOC was not going to resolve the problems, Riverkeeper filed a lawsuit in 2005. Our settlement included the removal of thirty truckloads of sediment from the wetlands by a bucket brigade of prison inmates, the planting of a small forest to stabilize a steep slope, and a conservation easement on eight acres to be protected in perpetuity.

A few days before Thanksgiving 2014, a rural landowner reported that a large volume of smelly, muddy water was flowing past his property near Mossy Creek in White County. Our staff tracked the discolored water as it flowed miles downstream into Hall County, where it entered the Chattahoochee at Mossy Creek State Park. Water samples revealed high bacteria levels—many times the federal limit for recreational waters. The cause? An abandoned two-acre waste lagoon at a hog farm had been intentionally breached with a backhoe by its new owner.

Six million gallons of bacteria-laden hog waste had spilled into Mossy Creek, not far from the river and the park. I called the publisher of the *White County News* to report the incident, which became front-page news over the holiday weekend. The state fined the perpetrator and forced him to implement an expensive restoration plan. We hoped the enforcement action and media attention would serve as a deterrent to owners of other abandoned hog ponds.

During most years, Riverkeeper and EPD log more calls from citizens concerned about damaged stream buffers and muddy water downstream of construction sites than any other complaint, perhaps because the pollution is so visible. According to EPD, polluted storm runoff is the major cause of impaired water quality in Georgia waters. Silt and sediment in runoff can choke the life out of streams (literally) and increase the cost of producing clean drinking water.

In 2005 Riverkeeper embarked on a campaign to evaluate the effectiveness of Georgia's erosion control programs, advocate for more effective regulations, and increase monitoring and site inspections. We also offered workshops for citizens, local governments, and developers. The program, Get the Dirt Out, has been highly effective in achieving its goals and has been replicated by other organizations regionally and nationally. Donahue Studios, owned by longtime Riverkeeper board member Denise Donahue, created outstanding Get the Dirt Out materials to engage and inform citizens, developers, and government regulators.

Riverkeeper's ability to collect and process water samples, essential for locating pollution sources, was limited during the organization's first decade. Monitoring technology at that time was not cost-effective for a small nonprofit. We relied on assistance where we could get it, often from federal environmental agencies or private consultants. Many generous people helped us pro bono or at reduced rates.

With greater technical expertise on staff, a larger budget, and advancing technologies, Riverkeeper commenced water monitoring programs in the late 2000s. These initiatives have helped tremendously in identifying where and how pollutants are impacting surface and ground waters in the Chattahoochee River basin. Streams are typically evaluated for excess nutrients, industrial toxins, sediment, or bacteria.

Neighborhood Water Watch (NWW)—the brainchild of current riverkeeper Jason Ulseth—is Chattahoochee Riverkeeper's community-driven and nationally acclaimed monitoring program. Trained volunteers sample bacteria levels in the river and tributaries weekly at more than two hundred sites. Their efforts have led to the discovery of hundreds of leaking sewers and other water quality problems, most of which have been satisfactorily resolved. To enhance volunteer safety, Jason—always focused and analytical—invented a practical device to collect water samples from bridges over waterways. These samplers, approved by the U.S. EPA and Georgia EPD, are being used around the country.

More than one hundred people are engaged in the NWW volunteer program today. Community member Bryan Jenkins explains: "This is an important thing to me. I didn't expect it to impact me this way. I took to this thing and absolutely enjoy sampling the water and bringing it back [to the Riverkeeper lab] to know what's in it. If it were not for us out here doing this, we wouldn't know half of what's going on in our river and waterways."

NWW has been empowering for the individuals who commit their time to caring for neighborhood streams. "You realize that nature is so resilient if we give it half a chance. Riverkeeper is one of the organizations that tries to give it half a chance," says veteran volunteer Alan Toney.

One watershed near downtown Atlanta has received more than half a chance, thanks to many individuals, foundations, government agencies, and organizations. Riverkeeper's primary contribution to this effort in recent years has been the bacteria monitoring program.

Rising from a spring on the heavily built and paved western edge of downtown Atlanta, the urban-industrial Proctor Creek watershed is one of the most intensively monitored streams in the state. During a drought in the early 1900s, a third of Proctor Creek's flow consisted of sewage; typhoid was rampant in the city. This nine-mile tributary to the Chattahoochee now has twenty NWW bacteria monitoring sites in its watershed, all installed and maintained by Riverkeeper.

Until 2008 the pipes in the city's combined storm and sewer system spilled untreated sewage and polluted stormwater dozens of times per year into Proctor Creek, a stream that flows through long-impoverished, now gentrifying, neighborhoods. Pursuant to Riverkeeper's consent decree with the city of Atlanta, more than $100 million was spent to repair and replace sewer infrastructure in this relatively small watershed.

The old pipes that moved storm runoff and untreated sewage together were reengineered in many places. Now, the runoff and the sewage flow through separate pipes to their destinations—either the river (runoff) or the treatment plant (sewage). In a portion of the system that was not separated, one outfall pipe into Proctor Creek has remained. It has not had a major overflow, as defined by federal law, in more than a decade. In the late 1990s, 132 tons of trash were removed from the creek and seventy acres of adjacent green space were permanently protected.

Despite these excellent results, Riverkeeper's monitoring data showed, in 2010 and subsequent years, that bacteria levels in Proctor Creek's headwaters near the Georgia World Congress Center were still high in some places. With more data, on-site investigations, and help from the nonprofit West Atlanta Watershed Alliance, the Riverkeeper team discovered that city contractors had failed to reroute thirty-plus underground sewer lines. One line served a large mall and another a university; the contents of the toilets flushed at these venues were still flowing straight into Proctor Creek and through neighborhoods.

It was not an easy task to find and fix every break and illicit connection, given that accurate city maps showing the location of underground pipes were scarce. Without original engineering and construction drawings, it's no wonder that city contractors failed to find all the illicit pipe connections in their initial work.

Persistent Riverkeeper staff and community volunteers ultimately identified the leaks, working alongside dedicated city employees. It took years—and more than $1 million—before Atlanta was able to stop the filthy discharges in portions of the Proctor Creek watershed where the city thought it had separated all of the sewage and storm runoff pipes.

Today, bacterial pollution in the creek's headwaters has been reduced by nearly 80 percent from 2010 levels, which were already exponentially lower than the pollution levels in the 1990s—before the city's decree-mandated investment in new infrastructure. Riverkeeper's investigative and problem-solving work continues with help from its loyal legion of dedicated volunteers.

Mikita Browning, Atlanta's current commissioner for the Department of Watershed Management, says that Riverkeeper and the city "forged a collaborative and positive bond, where they notify us when there are sewer overflows, or any water quality issues throughout the city system."

We had finally traveled the long, but important, distance from litigation to collaboration.

CHAPTER 17

Celebrating Milestones

November 6, 2019

> Remember to celebrate milestones as you prepare
> for the road ahead.
> —*Nelson Mandela*

Lucie Langford Canfield and Alice Franklin join me on the trail again for a late fall walk. We marvel at the hundreds, if not thousands, of slowly decomposing bigleaf magnolia leaves that dominate the forest floor. Lucie says that it looks like the morning after a huge party, before the cleaning crew arrives. Exactly!

I think of the many joyful celebrations that followed our victories on behalf of the Chattahoochee. Some of the more memorable of them marked the progress made to stop Atlanta's chronic sewage spills into the river and its tributaries.

The federal lawsuit Riverkeeper filed against the city of Atlanta in 1995 for its chronic sewage overflows—and then successfully settled with a consent decree—was a thread that ran through all my years with the organization. That thread continues today with my successors. The effort to overhaul the city's sewer system, one of its oldest and largest capital assets, was complex legally, technically, and politically.

Most of the city's sewer system was built between 1890 and 1930 on the abrupt slopes and narrow floodplains of an Appalachian forest. In 1934 construction began on a new city sewer system financed by the federal Works Progress Administration. Before that, half of all sewage was simply dumped into streams flowing into the Chattahoochee.

As Georgia Environmental Protection Division director Harold Reheis said in an interview in 2003, "The whole Chattahoochee . . . used to be septic, when I first started working here." Reheis was hired at the agency as a water engineer in 1969, a few years before Congress passed the Clean Water Act.

With each new home, hotel, and high-rise office building, the number of connections to the aging system increased. By the early 1970s—when Congress passed the Clean Water Act and authorized funding to build new municipal sewage facilities—Atlanta's system was already heavily overloaded. When it rained, untreated sewage poured directly into city creeks. Toilet paper dangled from overhanging trees. Human waste rotted in stagnant pools, even in city parks.

Massive sewage spills into the river and its tributaries were routine. Six hundred million gallons of smelly, discolored water entered waterways during just two events that occurred in the late 1980s. Environmental officials at government agencies knew about the situation, but they failed to take any significant action. The pollution worsened in the following decades. It became a growing threat to public health, recreational areas, and property values.

In several old and highly developed areas of the city, like the Proctor Creek watershed, rain that flowed from streets and other hard-surfaced areas into storm drains was funneled into one collection system. That system carried household, commercial, and industrial wastewater to treatment plants. During the torrential downpours with which Atlantans are so familiar, the sudden inflows of rainwater swamped the overtaxed pipeline collection system, and stormwater and sewage overflowed into creeks and rivers.

Around the country, more than one thousand other communities were also grappling with the overflows or spills from similar combined sewer systems, known as CSOs (combined sewer overflows). Built nearly one hundred years ago, Atlanta's combined sewer system carried wastewater and storm runoff from about fifteen percent of the city proper.

In the 1980s, the city developed a plan to deal with its CSOs; however, in the absence of any regulatory pressure from the state or federal governments, there was little political support from city leaders to move forward.

Federal involvement with municipal combined sewer systems did not occur until EPA developed a national strategy in 1989 and a policy in 1994. It required all states to develop permitting programs to reduce, eliminate, or control CSOs.

The disgusting and unhealthy situation outraged everyone. The affected Black neighborhoods, which have long suffered a disproportionate share of environmental problems in Atlanta and throughout America, were particularly aggrieved. Riverkeeper staff, board, and engineering consultants hired to help us evaluate the complex issues focused on the federal case. We were determined to force the city to comply with the Clean Water Act and achieve clean water standards in waterways by dates certain. Some neighborhood activists proposed alternative solutions to deal with the CSOs. (One ardent activist told me Riverkeeper's reputation and credibility would be harmed if we didn't support these solutions.)

The primary goal of these activists, as we came to understand it, was for all overflow pipes and other infrastructure at the CSO sites to be closed or removed from their communities. They also demanded all combined storm and sewage pipelines be separated; this included the lines deep underground in downtown Atlanta beneath dense development. Some were also opposed to any solution that included deep rock tunnels to transport and store the massive amounts of wastewater and storm runoff before treatment. Despite initial issues with cleaning debris from the tunnels that were ultimately built, they have performed well.

Given the ongoing failure in this country to fairly treat and involve all affected people in environmental decisions—regardless of their race, color, national origin, or income—the demands of these activists were understandable. Unfortunately, they were not achievable under existing federal law. The Clean Water Act was the only legal tool we had to demand that the city stop releasing raw sewage into the river. The law did not require the specific outcomes that the activists sought.

Even if the law had required such outcomes, the significant additional cost and burden on ratepayers, lengthy disruption of downtown businesses and neighborhoods from street closures, plus many additional years to complete the system upgrade were of great concern. Riverkeeper and our coplaintiffs sought the most practicable, cost-effective solutions to meet clean water laws in a timely manner. Finally, there was no certainty that the alternative proposals would be more effective in working toward cleaner streams and rivers. On the positive side, the activists convinced city officials to consider innovative wastewater treatment options and developed solutions to respond to long-standing problems facing neighborhoods near sewage plants, such as odor control.

Where it was technically and financially feasible, the city ultimately separated about eleven miles of combined sewers on its own initiative and at the urging of the activists. This reduced the total area served by the combined system to about 9 percent of the city proper by 2008. As Riverkeeper learned later through intensive monitoring work, pipe separation did not stop all sewage leaks. The Riverkeeper water monitoring team spent years finding, reporting, and resolving ongoing problems.

In the remaining 85 percent of the city that was not part of the combined system, frequent and illegal overflows from sanitary sewer pipes polluted neighborhood streams, even during dry weather. The city had failed to maintain, repair, and replace its nearly two thousand miles of sewer lines or upgrade its sewage treatment plants, which often malfunctioned.

The condition of the infrastructure essential to the economic prosperity of Atlanta and the health of its citizens and environment revealed a dereliction of duty. Over decades, city administrations had failed to invest in these critical systems, inevitably leading to the crisis.

After the partial separation of storm and sewer pipes in the combined areas was completed, storm runoff and trash continued to flow into creeks. There are few enforceable regulations that require technologies to control stormwater pollution. A stormwater utility, which would collect fees from property owners to manage storm runoff, would help Atlanta reduce trash and flooding. To date, however, the city has not mustered the political will to create a fee-based stormwater utility.

In recent years, Atlanta has worked with many partners to develop green infrastructure to protect, restore, or mimic the natural water cycle.

These practices include pervious paving, rain gardens, tree planting, and rainwater harvesting. The projects are helping to abate flooding and improve water quality. In 2013 the city updated its stormwater management ordinance with support from Riverkeeper and others to require green infrastructure on new development and redevelopment sites. Atlanta was the first jurisdiction in Georgia to adopt such a measure, which has come to serve as a model.

Fundamentally, it is difficult and expensive to manage the massive amounts of wastewater and stormwater generated by people, businesses, and storms in a dense urban area. Human error makes the task even more challenging. That said, Atlanta and other major cities must do more to protect people and natural systems. Climate change complicates the matter further, as intense and more frequent rainfall events increasingly burden city infrastructure.

What did the state of Georgia do about Atlanta's long-standing sewer crisis? In the late 1980s, Jack Dozier, Georgia EPD's Water Protection Branch chief, told the *Atlanta Journal-Constitution*'s environmental reporter Charles Seabrook that the state would not release to the public the results of water samples taken in city streams. He apparently feared someone might use the results to "embarrass" Atlanta.

The 1988 Democratic National Convention was set to take place in the city; Dozier and his colleagues may have been concerned about negative publicity. Alternatively, Dozier's reticence may simply have been attributable to the fact that EPD, as a government agency, has seldom been known for its transparency, cooperation, or collaboration with the public and nonprofits.

(Several years after Riverkeeper was established, a friendly EPD employee forwarded me an email from an EPD manager that read: "Today, Riverkeeper's attorney will be looking at draft permits [public documents]. . . . These visits are becoming more and more frequent and with these people camping out in our library within earshot of any conversations between EPD staff, I am becoming more and more tired of happily providing a ready source of income to these people." While the income reference may have been a snarky allusion to the attorney's fees that can arise from successful legal complaints, the basic message wasn't a surprise. EPD has long officially viewed—and described—the businesses and municipalities it regulates as its "customers," instead of the general public.)

At the meeting then-congressman Newt Gingrich called in 1988 after Charles Seabrook's explosive front-page story, Dozier denounced the media coverage as "overzealous reporting." The paper's headline: "Death by Pollution: Atlanta's Waste Choking the Life Out of West Point Lake."

Democrat Quillian Baldwin, a local state senator from LaGrange, challenged Seabrook, saying that he and others were "going to his editors." Not surprisingly, Seabrook, always a tough, principled reporter, responded: "Go ahead." With irrefutable data, federal and university scientists had already confirmed the facts about West Point Lake's condition and its likely future. Seabrook knew his story was accurate.

At that time, the prevailing attitude at Georgia's EPD was to ignore or downplay Atlanta's sewage crisis. As the agency's leaders often remarked, it would be "prohibitively expensive" for ratepayers to fund the infrastructure overhaul.

I often heard Dozier's boss, EPD Director Harold Reheis, say: "We don't want to take food off people's tables," apparently meaning that some environmental cleanups, including the repair and replacement of Atlanta's sewer system, were just too expensive to undertake. For the city's current and future prosperity and the health of its citizens and downstream communities, Riverkeeper believed that the massive project was too critical not to undertake.

Reheis and most of those who preceded and succeeded him as the head of EPD yield, too often, to political pressure from elected officials, even if only anticipated. The state legislators who vote annually on EPD's budget understand their power. These internal politics have never boded well for the state's environment or its people, as financially motivated special interest lobbyists prey on both legislators and state agencies.

By the early 1990s, the public was beginning to wake up to the serious water pollution issues, thanks largely to investigative reporters like Seabrook. Another newspaper headline in the *Atlanta Journal-*

Constitution from that time declared, "Streams of Waste: Atlanta's Economic Growth Depends on Its Ability to Save Its Urban Waterways."

When several attempts to resolve the sewage crisis without litigation failed, Riverkeeper and its allies filed their lawsuit against the city in 1995. Two years later, U.S. District Judge Thomas Thrash issued an order in our favor on a motion for summary judgment, finding that it was "a matter of undisputed fact that the CSO [combined sewer overflow] treatment facilities are dumping massive amounts of proscribed metals and fecal coliform into the tributaries of the Chattahoochee."

As a matter of law, the city had violated the Clean Water Act, and there was no need for a trial, according to the judge. His decision was of national importance. It was the first time a court had ruled that water quality standards applied to discharges from CSOs.

A few months later, EPA filed its companion action against the city with bipartisan political support from Newt Gingrich and Cynthia McKinney. Prepared by the U.S. Department of Justice, the lawsuit outlined additional clean water violations that EPA had uncovered several years earlier. Under pressure from EPA, the Georgia EPD joined the federal agency as a plaintiff in the action.

Judge Thrash's order led to months of intense negotiations among the parties to the litigation. Continuing to fight our efforts to force the city to stop polluting, Mayor Bill Campbell—who later spent sixteen months in federal prison for tax evasion—railed against our lawsuit and the judge's decision in the media. His administration spent significant taxpayer dollars making our settlement efforts more difficult.

Ultimately, a lengthy consent decree was negotiated, signed, and later amended to incorporate requirements associated with the EPA's complaint. The first section of the decree, signed in 1998, dealt with the combined portion of the city's sewer system, while the second section, which originated from EPA's action in 1999, covers the rest of the system: sanitary sewer lines and treatment plants.

Hundreds of pages in length, the document outlines data to be collected, studies to be undertaken, and vital compliance deadlines to be met over fifteen years. It would take time and a great deal of money—ultimately more than $2 billion—to overhaul the city's vast network of underground sewer pipes and aboveground sewage treatment facilities.

Shirley Franklin—the first Black woman to be elected mayor of a major southern city—became Atlanta's chief executive in 2002. She quickly learned the scope of the massive task ahead. Determined that the city not merely comply with the consent decree, she embraced its requirements. Franklin convened a panel of regional and national experts to advise her on the best solutions and established Clean Water Atlanta. The goal of this initiative, then and now, is "to ensure clean water for the next generation." She proudly dubbed herself the "sewer mayor."

Franklin's honesty, strategic actions, and willingness to take on roadblocks to a successful outcome were crucial. Those barriers included an obstructive Atlanta City Council and a recalcitrant federal government that refused to provide meaningful financial assistance.

On January 5, 2004, after an aggressive campaign led by Franklin and the business community, the council finally approved a substantial water and sewer rate increase, resulting in the highest rate in the country. It would help fund the critically needed system improvements. A motivating factor in the council vote was Franklin's last-resort notification to federal regulators and some state officials that the city was preparing to defy court agreements. In other words, the mayor was willing to risk being jailed along with the culpable council; she was that frustrated with the city's failure to resolve the sewer crisis.

A prominent business leader said that the city council action was possibly one of the most important votes in Atlanta's history. The city could not grow without adequate sewer and water capacity. Always focused on the city's long-term prosperity, Mayor Franklin included a much-needed overhaul of the city's aged drinking water system along with the legally mandated sewer fix. The total combined cost was estimated to be a whopping $3–4 billion, a sum significantly enlarged by the preceding decades of inaction and underinvestment in the city's infrastructure.

Two years later, still laser-focused on Atlanta's sewage and drinking water systems and fearless, Mayor Franklin said, "I am committed to the idea that clean drinking water and a functioning, environmentally-sound sewer system are vital to Atlanta's long-term development prospects. If that is my legacy, it is one I will be proud of."

Franklin also persuaded the Georgia legislature to pass a municipal option sales tax in Atlanta to share the cost of the sewer fix between residents, tourists, and those who work but do not live in the city—all of whom rely daily on dependable water and sewer systems. To this day, I count the former mayor as a friend and ally, in addition to admiring her for being such an effective public official and extraordinary politician.

The bigleaf magnolia "party leaves" my friends and I found on the forest floor at Cabin Creek reminded me of the many celebrations that marked the city's progress through the years to fix its plumbing system and clean up our waterways.

There was the impromptu celebration in 1997, when Judge Thrash's order in Riverkeeper's favor came unexpectedly—and nearly illegibly—through our office fax machine on the slick paper used at the time. There were celebrations with adult beverages a year later when we settled the case. The consent decree required a $2.5 million fine (one of the largest environmental fines imposed on a municipality at that time), two supplemental environmental projects that would cost the city $30 million to implement, and the mandated, multibillion-dollar upgrade for the city's entire sewer system.

In 1999 we applauded the city for completing the first of two required environmental projects. In a yearlong effort, every piece of trash was removed from thirty-seven miles of streams; 568 tons of man-made debris were pulled out of the water and dislodged from streambanks. Seven years later, we noted a major infrastructure milestone—the completion of an underground sewage storage and conveyance tunnel parallel to Nancy Creek. My sons humored me and participated in the festive New Year's Eve party held in the tunnel.

Later that year, we put on hard hats again and went several hundred feet below the streets of Atlanta to observe the excavation work completed by a massive boring machine nicknamed Rocksanne. She had dug a twenty-seven-foot diameter tunnel through granite, connecting sewer facilities four and a half miles apart.

We joined a large group of diverse supporters in 2003 to celebrate the purchase of more than 160 acres of mature forest and floodplain along Utoy Creek in southwest Atlanta. Funding for this multimillion-dollar acquisition was partially provided by the city's greenway acquisition program, the second environmental project required by our consent decree. Now known as Lionel Hampton–Beecher Hills Park, this protected green space, enlarged in subsequent years, rivals Atlanta's renowned Piedmont Park in size and history.

Several years later, I joined Mayor Franklin at an Earth Day event at the Trappist Monastery of the Holy Spirit, east of Atlanta, to celebrate a conservation easement on 137 acres secured with greenway funds. The easement purchase on land at the confluence of the South River and Honey Creek helped the monastery continue its work to purchase a larger adjacent tract for protection, now part of the Arabia Mountain National Heritage Area.

Completed in 2007, Atlanta's greenway acquisition program, required by our legal settlement, ultimately protected nearly two thousand acres of land in 150 parcels located in metro Atlanta and downstream communities. These properties must be maintained in a natural and undisturbed state to help safeguard rivers and streams from pollution: a grand legacy for future generations.

In 2008 Riverkeeper helped announce the completion of the biggest capital improvement sewer project—the West Side tunnel and other facilities; they would meet legal requirements to manage the combined storm and sewer system. The work was finished on time and under budget at a cost of $828 million. Some neighborhood activists who opposed the city's sewer plan had claimed the project would cost billions. No longer would at least four billion gallons of stormwater and sewage flow into streams and the river every year. Judge Thrash called it a "remarkable accomplishment."

By 2014 the city of Atlanta had completed all major capital improvement projects required under the consent decree. The Great Recession, exceptional drought, and other issues had pushed the deadline for final completion of some remaining projects to 2027; this was largely in order to spread out the costs to ratepayers.

Monitoring data revealed that 99 percent of the volume of untreated sewage flowing into the river in the 1990s had been stopped. More than one hundred miles of the river and tributaries were dramatically cleaner. People who lived and worked along the section of the river long impacted by the city happily reported that it looked and smelled cleaner.

Alan Cressler, an observant scientist with the U.S. Geological Survey, has monitored water quality in the Chattahoochee downstream of Atlanta for decades. "I couldn't believe it," he told me in 2011. "Although it's a common species and reportedly tolerant, I never thought that I'd find a southern rainbow mussel in the river below Atlanta. This is an indication to me that the cleanup effort was worth it."

For those focused on the city's economy, the news was extremely good. According to Mayor Franklin, the massive upgrade of critical sewer and water infrastructure resulted in private investments of at least $18 billion in the urban core. Developers were finally assured that the city's plumbing system could handle the wastewater from their new buildings. Sewer connection moratoriums for new construction were a thing of the past.

In an interview in 2014, Franklin said, "Clean water is essential to life. In Atlanta, we learned that lesson the hard way with a really—some would say *brutal*—suit against the city of Atlanta, but it resulted in a great outcome. I knew that had there not been a suit, had there not been a Sally Bethea, had there not been a board at the CRK [Chattahoochee Riverkeeper], the city of Atlanta would have dragged its feet for another fifty years."

Riverkeeper's twentieth-anniversary gala in 2014 recognized and thanked the individuals, companies, and foundations that had made this remarkable success possible. The next day, we went back to monitoring and advocating on behalf of the Chattahoochee. Environmental success depends on persistent vigilance, along with joyful celebrations.

As other major urban areas around the country grapple with their old, deteriorating water and sewer infrastructure—increasingly stressed by climate change—the city of Atlanta is nearly finished with its massive sewer system upgrades. At long last, the city also has proper maintenance and repair programs in place. Those programs must be adequately funded and managed every year to ensure that the city's infrastructure never again falls into such disrepair. The pipes and facilities that bring clean water to our homes and businesses and carry away wastewater and storm runoff are essential to public health and safety, economic prosperity, and a clean environment.

Nearly twenty-two thousand species of moss (*Bryophyta*), like these in the Chattahoochee River National Recreation Area, are distributed throughout the planet. Photo: Tom Wilson.

CHAPTER 18

Tainted Money

November 12, 2019

As I walk from my car to the Cabin Creek trailhead, a large group of crows—formally and poetically, a murder of them—flies over my head, cawing noisily to one another. Intelligent and clever tricksters with advanced communications skills, crows are thought by some cultures to bring good luck and by others to bring bad luck. I consider them a good omen for today's walk in the woods and am not disappointed.

Yellow leaves on hickory and beech trees dominate the palette of the forest, punctuated by swaths of once crimson, now pale watermelon-colored sourwood leaves. Tree trunks are dark, wet columns, soaked from a recent storm.

Stemflow is the term foresters use to describe the water that flows down tree trunks from their canopies when it rains. Leaves and twigs intercept raindrops, forming tiny rivulets at the confluence of smaller and then larger branches until the water reaches the trunk, where it's absorbed into the furrowed bark. Tributaries flowing into an arboreal river. Once the trunk is saturated, excess stemflow, containing valuable nutrients from leaves and bark, streams to the ground to be recycled by thirsty roots.

The air smells sweet and spicy from the earthy dampness and decomposing vegetation, as I descend the path to the creek. Decorating an old, decaying log are pear-shaped puffballs (*Apioperdon pyriforme*). They are considered an excellent edible mushroom when young and fresh but are not collectible in a national park without a permit.

On the ground, all color resides in the intensely green hue of the mosses: the most primitive and simple of land plants, with nearly twenty-two thousand species worldwide. With no flowers, fruits, seeds, roots, or internal vascular systems to conduct water, they have evolved with the rudimentary components of stem and leaf. Adapting to their shady lives under the forest canopy, mosses tolerate wild swings of moisture.

Practicing attentiveness, I search for the emerald microcommunities, each made up of hundreds of individual leaf stems. I find them everywhere. They are gleaming with water drops among piles of wet leaves, growing at the bottom of living trees, wrapping around tree stumps, carpeting the ground, and climbing rock outcrops. Kneeling, I touch and smell the tiny plants, really seeing them for the first time. With simple magnification, the patterns created by nature's weaving of the moss tapestries are visible and astonishing.

The miracle of photosynthesis is evident in the pure green color of these tiny plants. The moss leaves are silky-soft. Given some species' antibacterial properties, they have been used since ancient times to dress wounds. A sense of wonder and awe spark the desire for deeper knowledge. Nan Shepherd, one of Britain's greatest nature writers, wrote: "Knowing another is endless. The thing to be known grows with the knowing. The mind cannot carry away all that it has to give."

In her book *Gathering Moss,* Robin Wall Kimmerer notes that mosses must rely primarily on Latin names, rather than common names, such as those given to trees and flowers. There are so many of them and so few known to the public. She believes in the power of naming as an intimate way of gaining deeper knowledge.

"Having words for these forms makes the differences between them so much more obvious. With words at your disposal, you can see more clearly. Having words also creates an intimacy with the plant that speaks of careful observation. Intimacy gives us a different way of seeing." Kimmerer concludes, "Knowing their names is the first step in regaining our connection."

Using a nature app on my smartphone, I find common names for some of the mosses that inhabit the Cabin Creek ravine: tree skirt moss (*Anomodon attenuatus*), spoon-leaved moss (*Bryoandersonia illecebra*), fern moss (*Thuidium delicatulum*), broom forkmoss (*Dicranum scoparium*), and pincushion moss (*Leucobryum glaucum*). These wonderful names help me see these patient plants as the individuals they are, not just luscious, nameless clumps of bright green.

Green—the color of life, renewal, and fertility—symbolizes the natural world. It is also associated with money. My riverkeeping years underscored the meaning, and importance, of both interpretations.

Without significant financial support, Riverkeeper would not be able to revive and defend our river. Of that fact, I am certain. At the same time, donor solicitation and management can be complicated and tricky pursuits. Our board and staff always considered the sources of our funding, guided by our mission and core values, as we built our organization.

Over the years, when I was introduced as the riverkeeper for the Chattahoochee, people would often give me blank or puzzled looks. The new acquaintance clearly wondered what that word, *riverkeeper*, meant. The looks were followed by predictable questions. Is that a full-time job? Are you paid? Do you spend all your time in a boat on the river?

I would explain that managing and growing a private nonprofit is like running a business. The work we do requires expertise in many areas: environmental science, law, education, planning and policy making, water monitoring, public affairs, technology, boating, community organizing, media relations, fundraising, financial management, and more.

While volunteers and pro bono specialists provide important and much-appreciated support, Riverkeeper must also employ necessary expertise and fairly compensate staff members and contractors. As the organization grew, along with the scope and impact of its programs, the operation required more of my time off the water than on. And more money.

In its first year, Riverkeeper spent less than the fifty-thousand-dollar seed grant provided by the Turner Foundation to get the organization off the ground, supporting one full-time staff person in donated office space. Today, the organization's annual budget is approximately $2 million, and the staff has grown to eighteen people in three offices. Funds are raised from individuals, private foundations, businesses, and government agencies; in earlier years, Riverkeeper was the grateful beneficiary of rock music concerts, including a radio station's annual Jerry Jam.

After I retired in 2014, Juliet Cohen—our enterprising general counsel for many years—became Riverkeeper's executive director, expertly managing and enhancing the organization's operations. Notably, she successfully led and completed our first capacity-building campaign, working closely with the board. More than $2 million was raised for new programs and equipment—a huge endeavor that is taking the organization to the next level of impact in its third decade.

When I became Riverkeeper's first executive director and riverkeeper, I had limited experience in fundraising, but I learned quickly from our strategic and connected cofounders—Rutherford and Laura Turner Seydel. It helped tremendously that we were all passionate and had a compelling mission: enough clean water for families, communities, and ecosystems.

Riverkeeper appreciated early support from a wide range of foundations and companies, many with conservative views. They understood, then and now, that a clean environment is essential for a vibrant economy. While these donors rarely supported our legal actions, they applauded our persistence. The need for our work was underscored by regular media attention to the plight of Atlanta's drinking water supply, the frequent recipient of untreated sewage and other pollutants.

Leadership from Rutherford, Laura, and the entire Turner family guided and connected us to people with ideas and resources, as did other Riverkeeper board members through the years. Their collective dedication to our mission, their knowledge, and their commitment to good governance strengthened our organization immeasurably.

Essential to Riverkeeper's success is the fact that the board and staff are absolutely clear about the organization's mission and basic strategies. Riverkeeper has one overriding goal: a clean and healthy Chattahoochee River and watershed for everyone. All who support that goal in any way are welcome to join the team.

If an individual, business, or foundation wants to make a donation, Riverkeeper will gladly take it. The funds will be put to good use to protect and restore the river. If a donor wants to restrict a contribution to a project that is not a Riverkeeper priority—or does not coincide with the organization's core values—it politely declines the offer. Riverkeeper works hard to gain the public's trust through ethical standards and responsible practices.

Riverkeeper never developed a litmus test to evaluate potential donors in terms of the impacts of their business operations or positions on our mission. I'm not sure that level of analysis is even possible in the complex world in which we live. In truth, no individual or entity is totally "pure"; we all have varying impacts on the natural environment, some more intrusive and offensive than others.

Patrick Noonan, a highly successful former president of the Conservation Fund, known to be a strong fundraiser, has said, "The problem with tainted money is there t'aint enough." Some are offended by this viewpoint, while others consider it a practical reality. If an individual or entity wants to fund Riverkeeper's general operations or a specific priority project, then the organization is happy to be the recipient of their generosity.

Whether or not a proposed contribution from a problematic donor could be considered "tainted money" is a job for the board to decide, if necessary. That decision would be based on the context, situation, and parties involved. Riverkeeper is careful and strategic with invitations to join its policy-making board. It's too easy for an organization to evolve into a less robust, even compromised, version of itself as time passes. We do not want that to ever happen to Riverkeeper.

In the late 1990s, marketing executives from the Coca-Cola Company asked me if Riverkeeper would support a new bottled drinking water project by confirming that the Chattahoochee was not a reliable water supply. My answer was an easy one. Riverkeeper takes actions to ensure the Chattahoochee River serves as a clean and abundant supply of water for everyone at a reasonable price, available from their home faucets. Riverkeeper would not help promote bottled water. Coca-Cola respected that position, and a collaborative relationship between Riverkeeper and the company continues to this day.

As we walked near the river in the mid-2000s, a Georgia Power representative suggested to me in a private conversation that his company could "help us more" if Riverkeeper stopped speaking out in hearings at the state capitol. The representative didn't clarify the specific testimony that troubled him, but I had recently spoken against an unpopular bill related to the abuse of property rights through the use of eminent domain by utilities and governments. I wondered if that might be the cause of his concern. He did not say exactly how his company could help us more, but the implication was fairly obvious. This answer, too, was easy: "No, thank you."

Another donor-related issue arose in regard to Atlanta sewers. Several neighborhood activists accused me of accepting contributions for Riverkeeper from companies that might benefit financially from the city's chosen technology to upgrade its infrastructure. Guided by engineering consultants Riverkeeper hired and paid, the organization supported the city's plan based on its merits. Along with state and federal agencies, Riverkeeper had made recommendations to improve the plan, which were accepted.

I was upset by this spurious claim, which challenged my integrity and that of our organization, but I kept my head down as much as possible. I kept moving forward, focused on the facts, science, and ensuring enough clean water for everyone.

CHAPTER 19

Getting Booted from the Board

November 19, 2019

It actually doesn't take much to be considered a difficult woman. That's why there are so many of us.
—Jane Goodall

Most of the deciduous trees in the ravine have lost their leaves. It is possible to see much farther into the woods and up the steep slopes that rise from Cabin Creek. Trunks, large limbs, and branches that were largely hidden in the green forest tunnel of summer are now on display in all their structural glory.

I love the woods in winter and walk with my neck craned to admire for the first time the graceful, high branches: the canopy architecture of oaks, beeches, hickories, and magnolias. The irregular and expressive lines of nature never fail to stimulate my eyes and mind in ways that man's angular shapes and straight lines cannot.

Distant highway noise is louder now, given the fewer leafy barriers between my ears and the sound of fast cars and groaning trucks on asphalt. In the woods and at the water are wonderful cool, fresh smells. I find more purple gentians near the river and a birdhouse hanging over the water. Was it placed there by someone, or did it float downstream and catch on the branch during a storm when the water was high? No one seems to be home.

The fall colors of the trees beside the clear, low water are spectacular: bright yellow leaves that dazzle in the setting sun. Squirrels dart across the leaf-strewn ground as I walk back uphill to my car, energized and refreshed, encountering only a few people along the way. On walks like today's, I often wonder why I didn't allow myself to spend more time along the Chattahoochee during the two decades I was riverkeeping. It would have helped reduce the stress that accompanied my job almost daily.

During my seven years on the Georgia Board of Natural Resources, that stress increased exponentially. Being an advocate for nature on this board, where I was considered by some a difficult woman, was a lonely assignment. My memories of those years are illustrative.

In the winter, when the vegetation along the riverbank dies back, it's easy to see the metal and concrete outfall pipes that poke from the earth with their round orifices extending over the water. Some of these conduits discharge treated wastewater from sewage plants and industrial facilities, authorized by state permits. They operate year-round, using our waterways as repositories for the byproducts of human and economic activity. Other pipes and culverts discharge into the river and creeks only during and after storms, when runoff from the land is channeled into them to reduce flooding and is transported to the river.

Rivers are able to naturally assimilate some pollutants, depending on their size, the nature of the waste, and other discharges nearby. The federal Clean Water Act lays out the requirements for wastewater treatment and establishes a system for permits that must be obtained by cities and industries prior to disposing their treated waste in public waters. State and federal environmental agencies are responsible for enforcing the provisions in these permits.

Without signs on the pipes that discharge treated waste, fishers and boaters in Georgia had no idea what was being emptied into the waters where they recreated. If they saw something that appeared to be a problem, such as dead fish or discolored water near a discharge pipe, they didn't know who to contact.

Around the country, a few states had passed "fishermen's right to know" laws by the early 2000s, requiring cities and industries to place signs at their outfall pipes with basic information: permit number, nature of the discharge, and an emergency phone number. Senator Charles Walker, a Democrat from Augusta, tried to pass a similar bill in Georgia with support from the environmental community in the early 2000s. The legislation died after strong opposition from the Georgia Chamber of Commerce, Georgia Textile Manufacturers Association, and others.

Former congressman Lindsay Thomas, the head of the state chamber at the time, and other industry lobbyists said that putting signs on discharge pipes would "harm the traditional industries of Georgia." Further, they argued the signage would make these industries vulnerable to trespass, misleading photo ops, bad public relations, graffiti, and even industrial espionage.

The permits issued to these industries and municipalities legally allow them to use public waters for the disposal of their treated waste, as long as they meet required standards. The signs would simply help river users report and solve potential problems. What really worried these industries?

Crises often serve as the catalysts for policy change. Congress passed the Clean Water Act in the early 1970s after photos of the burning Cuyahoga River in Ohio and a major oil spill in California's Santa Barbara Channel captured the public's attention. A tipping point had been reached.

In Macon, Georgia, in 2001, a series of high-volume spills from the city's old and failing sewer system caused an outcry that reached the ears of Ben Porter, an influential member of the Georgia Board of Natural Resources and a resident of Macon. Like the people in the affected neighborhoods, he was outraged, and he proposed that the board adopt a new rule strengthening the reporting of sewage spills statewide. Signs would be required to notify the public of places that were contaminated when sewage pipes overflowed. As a leading member of the business-friendly majority on the board, Porter easily secured support for his proposal.

The sign discussions occurred during my years on the board. As the only card-carrying environmentalist on this decision-making body, my recommendations were rarely embraced by the pro-business, conservative majority. The initiative from the Macon board member presented an opportunity. I suggested that we also require the permanent labeling of all wastewater discharge pipes, as an expansion of the proposed rule requiring signage for sewer spills.

The board agreed to consider my proposal after a stakeholder process. During the lengthy meetings that followed, the state chamber and business leaders continued to rail against having to disclose information about their legally permitted discharges into public waters. While the chamber leaders won on the size of the signs—they wanted them to be as small as possible—the waterways of Georgia prevailed, as did the fishers and boaters who love them. Georgia became the fifth state in the country to enact these important right-to-know requirements.

In 2006, a few months before the end of my term on the board, Governor Sonny Perdue was running for reelection. The Republican had beaten Democratic governor Roy Barnes in an upset election in 2002. Perdue asked me and Laura and Rutherford Seydel to meet with him at the annual Weekend for Wildlife fundraising event to discuss my reappointment to the board.

I was not thrilled about being appointed to another seven-year term on the board. The monthly meetings could be very stressful for me as I attempted to bring fact-based arguments to the discussions. My perspective centered on the need to safeguard the state's valuable natural assets—soil, water, forests, minerals, and wildlife. Too often I felt I was unsuccessful.

While most of the board members were generally pleasant when we communicated, and some became friends, others exhibited an air of dismissiveness and condescension toward me. It had become quite wearing, really maddening, over time. Was it because I was an environmentalist or a woman? Both, I assumed, based on my many years of working in male-dominated settings.

One board member in particular, the head of a large property management company, was especially rude to me during the meetings, which were open to the public. While his bullying was not aimed at me exclusively, Tom Wheeler seemed to relish the chance to attack me whenever I asked a question or made a comment. Smiling and using my best Junior League voice, I once asked him during a board meeting to please stop being so rude to me. He didn't.

Wheeler was one of several people who became particularly annoyed when I had the temerity (in their view) to ask clarifying questions of Senator Chip Pearson when he appeared before us at a meeting. Pearson—the senator who had declared that a highly qualified scientist could not be trusted because she was a Riverkeeper board member—had, in my opinion, misrepresented a piece of legislation in his comments to the board. It concerned the perennial topic of stream buffers.

I couldn't let Pearson's characterization of this issue remain unchallenged. Again, using my nicest southern lady voice, I questioned the senator's information as politely as possible. My comments created quite a stir, I was told later, and no small amount of unhappiness among some board members and state officials. Others were delighted that the senator had been corrected.

My role and responsibilities on this board and my daily work on behalf of Riverkeeper demanded a great deal of me both intellectually and emotionally. I had to be tough, clear, factual, and persistent—attributes appreciated in men, but not so much in women. Not outspoken as a young adult, and shy as a child and teenager, I had to overcome these natural inclinations to become an effective advocate. Rather, I had to learn how to be emotional and tough: a duality often hard for colleagues and friends, and even myself, to grasp.

I may cry when I am very sad or concerned, but particularly when I am angry. Understanding how to embrace the mosaic of my emotions has been a long but largely fruitful journey. After all, emotions are what make us human. I've learned that truth, science, and emotion can build strong cases for positive environmental outcomes. Truth, especially, is always the enemy of power.

In the early 2000s, when Roy Barnes was still governor, colleagues working on environmental and health issues related to air pollution sought my advice on how best to present their concerns to the board. Specifically, they wanted the board to agree to hold additional public hearings around the state to allow citizens and experts to present testimony on power plant permits.

I urged my colleagues to meet with each board member individually to explain their concerns and their request, then present to the full board. They followed through on these suggestions. None of the board members they spoke with voiced opposition to holding additional hearings.

At a committee meeting that preceded the full board meeting, the clean air advocates testified and asked for the additional hearings. When the vote was taken, the majority of the committee members raised their hands against holding more hearings. I was livid. Tears flowed. It was so frustrating that these meetings were routinely rigged to protect those with power and money.

At the full board meeting the next day, the committee chair asked for another vote on the hearing matter. Surprisingly, it was approved and the public hearings were ultimately held. One longtime observer believes that Governor Barnes, a strong conservationist, had told the board members to allow the hearings to take place. Georgia's natural environment would have benefited significantly from a second Barnes term. That was not to happen.

Despite the personal challenges I faced as a board member, I was willing to reenlist for a second term. An environmental perspective on this board is vitally needed. The meeting with Governor Perdue and the Seydels in 2006 was cordial; he said he'd like to reappoint me. With some trepidation, I agreed.

Within a few days, the governor's chief of staff contacted me. He said that my reappointment was contingent upon my signing an undated resignation letter. It would be kept in a drawer, in case they needed to use it. In case I asked an inappropriate question? In case I voted the "wrong" way? He didn't say. I didn't ask. I signed the letter, confident that I was the only appointee, or reappointee, on the board who was required to execute such a document. I was also confident that I was not going to change my behavior. Sonny Perdue was reelected in November.

The Georgia Board of Natural Resources is among the many state boards whose governor-appointed members must secure state senate approval during the legislative session following the appointment. This confirmation is "generally an easy process," according to the state's website.

On April 19, 2007, at the end of the session that followed my reappointment to the board, Senate Majority Leader Tommie Williams, chair of the committee on assignments, walked to the front of the senate chamber. His task was to make a motion to approve the governor's long list of appointments to state boards and commissions. It contained hundreds of names.

Observers later said they noticed a good deal of paper-shuffling and conversation around Senator Williams before he called for a voice vote of approval. Shortly after the unanimous vote, several senators—apparently unable to contain their joy—bragged to the media present. One name had been removed from the list in the shuffle prior to the vote. Mine.

When asked why they booted me off the board, Senator Williams said they removed me because I was a lobbyist registered with the State Ethics Commission. He claimed that registered lobbyists could not sit on state boards, pursuant to a new law. That law was not applicable to my situation.

Ironically or not, Georgia being a conservative, pro-business state, other board members routinely voted on matters that could benefit their own personal finances, connected to the power industry, real estate investments, poultry, agriculture, and timber. They also routinely fail to register their activities.

I lobbied on behalf of Georgia's natural resources, registered as required by law, and was penalized, even though I didn't lobby for a business whose activities are regulated by the state. The stir in the media and among the general public in opposition to my being removed from the board lasted more than a month.

In an op-ed to the *Atlanta Journal-Constitution*, former governor Roy Barnes wrote, "Bethea's non-confirmation was not the result of a serious advise and consent role of the state Senate, but rather the work of lobbyists who did not wish to answer some of the tough questions she posed about the safeguarding of our natural resources." Others noted the selective enforcement aspect of the law regarding lobbyists. At the same time that I was booted from the board, the senate approved other registered lobbyists to state boards.

I remembered the rumors about the disgruntled landowner with property on the Upper Chattahoochee Water Trail. He had supposedly asked then–lieutenant governor Casey Cagle, who presided over the state senate, to remove me from the board. I also thought about my friend and mentor Ogden Doremus. I wished that I could talk to him about this latest maneuver to stifle pro-environment voices. He had died several weeks earlier in a nursing home in South Georgia, a month before his eighty-sixth birthday.

A dedicated environmentalist, brilliant lawyer, lobbyist, and judge who fittingly was born on Earth Day (April 22), Ogden had pushed me hard, as he pushed everyone, to have the courage to speak out and not allow "the bastards" to defeat us—the bastards being polluters and their many handlers. Ogden was not a patient man, to say the least, and his mentorship wasn't easy, but he helped me find the resolve and develop skills to speak truth to power. He was a deeply loyal friend.

Beginning in the early 1950s, Ogden had fought successfully to keep sewage out of rivers, protect coastal marshlands, and preserve the rights of citizens to safeguard their communities. As a member of the Atlanta Board of Aldermen, now the Atlanta City Council, he successfully lobbied for a state law to stop sawmills from dumping waste into Peachtree Creek, a major tributary to the Chattahoochee. In 1996 the Georgia House passed a resolution honoring him for his work on the Coastal Marshlands Protection Act and dubbed him "Mr. Environment."

Sara Clark, an admired, conservation-minded member of the Board of Natural Resources who served a term as its chair, attempted to have Ogden recognized for his many contributions. She thought he deserved the state's highest conservation award: the R. L. "Rock" Howard Award, named for the respected first director of the Georgia EPD.

Before Sara's nomination could be seriously considered, it was quashed. A new candidate was rushed forward for approval. The business-as-usual authorities within Georgia's Department of Natural Resources, and their elected overseers, apparently could not stomach honoring anyone who had successfully pushed them to do a better job of protecting the state's air, land, and water.

I recently looked at my file of news stories from that time, along with notes from friends, colleagues, and strangers. All expressed outrage that the "strongest pro-environment voice" on the board had been sacked so unceremoniously, for such a trumped-up reason. Many realized that with the departure within the previous six months of three other conservation-minded individuals, and now my dismissal, the board had completed a historic changeover. No longer did a single member of the board have a science, natural resources, or environmental policy background. Although we four represented a small minority on the board, evidently just hearing differing opinions during discussions was too much for Georgia's growth-at-any-cost boosters to tolerate.

Five years later, Governor Nathan Deal declined to reappoint Warren Budd, a lifelong Republican and "Teddy Roosevelt conservationist," to the board. Budd had expressed skepticism about Deal's proposals to dam rivers to build reservoirs. He had also criticized the state's small fine for a textile company that caused the largest fish kill in Georgia history. Budd explained to a reporter: "I was told to hush up on both of them. I was warned and I didn't do it, and that's why I'm off."

Today, the Georgia Board of Natural Resources has nineteen members appointed by Republican governors: fifteen white men, one Indian American man, one Venezuelan American man, and two white women. Following decades of "tradition," this board, whose decisions affect the health and prosperity of every Georgian and our natural environment, does not come close to reflecting the demographics of our growing and diversifying state.

CHAPTER 20

Is the Water Safe to Swim?

December 2, 2019

Randy joins me on today's walk to the river. The Cabin Creek ravine is fully exposed with its dramatic topography; the contours of the land and rocky outcrops are on display. We scuffle through the deep piles of decaying leaves that now cover the forest floor and our path.

I notice that leaves cling tenaciously to the branches of young American beeches (*Fagus grandifolia*). These juvenile trees, largely invisible in the forest from spring to fall, now dominate the winter woods. Light brown and curled, looking like ornaments made of parchment paper, the beech leaves shimmer on this windy day, making rustling, musical sounds.

The beech leaves are beautiful. I can't stop watching them move. How is it possible that I have never noticed them before? The horizontal layers of leaf-decorated branches on each young tree twist and turn like layered skirts of twirling dancers.

All living trees shed their leaves at some time, but there is great variation in the timing of leaf fall. At one end of the spectrum are the evergreens, which drop some of their old leaves and needles every few years; their predecessors, primitive conifers, appeared in ancient forests around 250 million years ago. On the other end are deciduous hardwoods, which typically drop their leaves all at once every fall. They appeared about one hundred million years after the conifers and diversified as today's continents began to form and drift apart. Early broad-leaved trees were oaks, maples, willows, laurels, and magnolias.

Between evergreens and deciduous trees is a middle ground best represented by beeches and some oaks, which are related. When the leaves on these trees die, they are not always shed until late winter or early spring, especially on young trees and on lower branches. The term for this retention of dead plant material is *marcescence* (to wither). Among forest scientists, theories abound as to why leaf marcescence occurs.

The retention of leaves may offer a means of protecting the nutritious new buds and twigs, especially on lower branches, from browsing animals like deer and from winter weather. The organic material may be useful to nourish the beech in the spring, when the leaves finally fall to the ground. It could provide a way to collect snow for spring meltwater to sustain the tree. Or it could simply be a sign that beech trees are evolutionarily delayed. No one knows for sure, as scientific research continues.

One of the most valuable tree species for wildlife, slow-growing American beech trees can reach heights of eighty feet and live more than three hundred years. Their smooth, gray bark is very thin and looks like skin. Natural fissures on the trunks create eerie eye-shaped marks. With the living tissue so close to the surface, it scars easily, as when the trees are carved with names and initials or scratched by animal claws.

Parasitic plants called beechdrops (*Epifagus virginiana*) appear under mature beech trees in late summer and fall. These foot-high, branched wildflowers with tiny, light tan and purple-tinged blooms produce no chlorophyll; they must obtain sugars and nutrients by attaching themselves to beech roots. Most of the year, they exist as underground roots. The only purpose of the aboveground stalk and flowers is to produce seeds.

Continuing our walk, I notice the graceful, arching stems and dark green leaves of mountain doghobble, another species that is largely lost in the abundance of summer vegetation. It is now visually dominant alongside the streams in the ravine. At the bottom of Devils Race Course Shoals, dozens of geese appear motionless in the water, the fast-moving current swirling around them. Randy and I can walk closer to the river in places where thick vegetation has now died back with the cooler temperatures.

Dog leash in one hand and trash bag in the other, I direct Randy back uphill. Nearing the trailhead and not paying attention to the uneven ground, I fall flat on my face, tripping over a leaf-covered root. With a bloody lip and an anxious dog, I limp back to the car. The black eye and dent in my nose appear later. Nature sleuthing is not as safe as it might seem.

My walks regularly spurred me to research the fascinating things I found at the river and in the woods, such as beech trees' retention of leaves during the winter. Science is a powerful tool in helping us understand the way the natural world works. With that knowledge, better decisions can be made to manage the environment as sustainably as possible.

When I started my riverkeeping career, I was acutely aware of all the things I didn't know but needed to understand to do my job. Thankfully, there were many individuals, organizations, universities, and government agencies available to guide me. One of the first agencies I approached was the U.S. Geological Survey (USGS), whose motto is "Science for a changing world."

Established in 1879, USGS studies the country's landscape, its natural resources, and the natural hazards that threaten it. The agency's reports on the Chattahoochee River basin, its ongoing data collection programs, and its willingness to answer our questions helped me and Riverkeeper staff better understand the river. Without this top-quality and timely scientific information, we would have been much less effective advocates.

"Is the water in the river safe for recreation?" People asked this question everywhere I went. I didn't have a scientifically based answer. In the late 1990s, the Clinton administration created the Partnership for Regional Livability to promote collaboration among government agencies such as USGS and the private sector. Meetings were convened with these agencies and several nonprofit organizations. At one of the gatherings, everyone agreed that the quality and safety of the water within the Chattahoochee River National Recreation Area needed to be evaluated. The public wanted to know if the water was safe to fish, boat, and swim.

Media coverage of the chronic sewage overflows polluting the river understandably worried people. They wondered about the condition of the entire river system. The notion that pollution in one section of the Chattahoochee meant the waterway was polluted for its whole length needed to be examined and explained. Data would be essential.

USGS, National Park Service, and Riverkeeper offered to lead the effort to create a BacteriALERT Monitoring Program, secure funding, and collect daily water samples from three locations in the park. Beginning in 2000, Riverkeeper staff and interns collected, refrigerated, and delivered samples to the USGS office for analysis. The agency posted results on its website. Ed Martin, a former Georgia district chief for USGS and one of the architects of the BacteriALERT Program, lauded the program. He said it was "the best example I know of the positive, worthwhile and effective programs that can be accomplished when agencies and stakeholders work together."

More than twenty years later, this successful partnership remains in operation, testing the waters and informing the public. The public can review quality-assured data online, along with user-friendly explanations. This long-running program is the only source of current, accurate bacteria data for people who recreate in the national park—and it's available thanks to dedicated teamwork by all of the participants.

In one humorous incident we laughed about for years, a fire engine roared to a stop one morning at a bridge over the river. Riverkeeper staffer Alice Champagne was taking a sample using a rope to drop the water collector into the river. A passing driver had called 911, worried that she might be trying to jump and take her life. Alice assured the firemen that she was not trying to harm herself and then gave them a lesson in river monitoring.

While the long-term data has revealed that bacteria levels in the river during normal and dry weather periods are much lower than expected— safe for healthy individuals—the levels can be high immediately after major storms. When it rains, the aging and broken sewer pipes and manholes that carry our waste can overflow with untreated sewage that pollutes nearby waterways, along with dirty storm runoff from urban areas.

A good rule of thumb is to avoid river recreation (certainly swimming) within a day or two after a heavy storm or when the water is very muddy. Because most bacteria prefer to live in warm animals rather than cold river water, microorganisms typically die off within three to five days after it rains.

Science, data, and rigorous analysis, the key components of our BacteriALERT Monitoring Program, answered an important question about the river.

About 140 miles downstream of the Chattahoochee River National Recreation Area, in Columbus, Georgia, Riverkeeper became concerned about potential threats to the health of people recreating in the river; a section of the river in the city is a nationally recognized whitewater venue.

After years of planning and permitting, in 2012, Columbus removed two historic mill dams to create two and a half miles of class III rapids (irregular waves, strong currents) and a state-of-the-art kayak surf wave. The project was an immediate success for watersport enthusiasts of all skill levels. While Riverkeeper has supported the venue, the organization was also aware that Columbus Water Works (cww), the utility that manages the region's wastewater and drinking water systems, had not done enough to upgrade its combined stormwater and sewage system with possible consequences for the river.

Our water monitoring data indicated there was a potential problem. Polluted stormwater and partially treated sewage appeared to be entering the river along the whitewater course when it rained. For years, state and federal environmental agencies had tried to compel cww to agree to a discharge permit for its combined system with bacteria and chlorine standards, just like every other municipality in Georgia.

The Georgia Environmental Protection Division issued a new permit to cww in 2020 with tougher limits on bacteria and chlorine released into the river. The water utility challenged the proposed permit in state court, saying its releases did not pollute the river and that the cost to comply would be too much.

Collaborating for the first time in our history, Riverkeeper joined EPD to defend the state's permit. Our mutual goal is to protect the Chattahoochee and the thousands of people who fish, boat, and swim in the river year-round. Five years of river monitoring data taken by Riverkeeper near one of the discharge points had revealed high levels of bacteria, underscoring the need for system improvements.

Attorneys with Southern Environmental Law Center expertly represented our case in court, working closely with the Riverkeeper team. In 2021 a state administrative law judge found in our favor, upholding the stronger EPD permit. cww appealed the judge's decision to the local superior court. We won again in 2022. cww appealed again, this time to the Georgia Court of Appeals; a hearing will be scheduled in 2023. The battle to protect the public and the river with laws and scientific data continues.

"Are the fish in the Chattahoochee safe to eat?" Another important query and another need for science and data. Within an industrialized area of the Chattahoochee, immediately downstream of Atlanta and the Chattahoochee River National Recreation Area, we routinely saw anglers with fish stringers as we patrolled the river.

Aware that the state had issued risk-based fish consumption guidelines for this river section, we worried they might be eating their catches. Mercury and PCBS—a synthetic chemical and banned carcinogen once used in electrical equipment—had been found in fish tissue. Persistent in the environment for decades, PCB remnants still settle into water and bind to sediments; they are consumed by small organisms, eventually accumulating in fish and animals.

Were the fishers ignoring state guidelines? Were they even aware of the recommendations? We subsequently learned that the guidelines were printed only in English and that they were provided only when fishing licenses were purchased. Did some of these anglers, many of whom were Black, Asian, or Hispanic, lack the literacy to interpret the guidelines? Were some of them fishing without licenses—meaning they hadn't received the guidelines at all? We were particularly concerned about pregnant and nursing women who might eat the fish. Data was needed to help us determine what actions to take.

Collaborating with the University of Georgia's River Basin Center, Riverkeeper conducted a multiyear survey in the target area to determine if the anglers were supplementing their families' diets with the fish they caught. Our study revealed that Black, Hispanic, and Asian fishers were twice as likely to consume their fish as white anglers.

This new information led to a collaborative project between Riverkeeper and Randy Manning with the Georgia Department of Natural Resources: the creation of simple guides to fish consumption printed in both English and Spanish. The brochures were distributed to Women, Infants, and Children clinics in metro Atlanta. (Years later, I learned that the current riverkeeper, Jason Ulseth, helped produce the fish consumption guides. He was an intern with Manning long before he became Riverkeeper's technical programs director. Serendipity!)

DNR continues to issue fish consumption advisories for sections of the Chattahoochee River and other waterways. They urge anglers to be informed about the kind, size, and quantity of fish they eat. It's uncertain when, or if, persistent chemical toxins like PCBS will finally disappear from the environment.

～ℓℓℓ～

Farther upstream on Lake Lanier, easily the most important reservoir in the state, Riverkeeper continues to play an important role in collecting and evaluating water quality data. This information helps guide policy making, permit issuance, and local land-use decisions in the reservoir's watershed.

In 1990 then–state senator Roy Barnes spearheaded legislation requiring EPD to set lake standards for phosphorus and nitrogen. He wanted to safeguard the lake for fishing, swimming, and drinking water. In 2000 standards for chlorophyll *a* (the green pigment essential for photosynthesis) were established at five locations in the lake to measure and manage algae growth. When the Georgia Board of Natural Resources approved these standards, EPD director Harold Reheis committed to monitor the reservoir and report back to the board in "a few years."

(A precedent-setting win at the Georgia Supreme Court in 2004—led by environmental attorney and Riverkeeper board member Steve O'Day—forced Gwinnett County to improve the quality of its treated wastewater. The court held that the county's discharge into Lake Lanier must meet the state's chlorophyll standards to keep lake waters clean, confirming the importance of these measures.)

Six years after the lake standards were adopted, EPD had still not evaluated the data collected, verified the accuracy of model predictions, revisited the standards, or presented this material to the board, as promised. Riverkeeper staff reviewed the state's monitoring data. We discovered that standards had been exceeded at one or more of the sites in three out of five years.

Not only had EPD failed to take any specific actions based on this information, but the agency also denied that the data indicated noncompliance. State employees promoted a convoluted interpretation of the standard exceedance methodology. With technical support from EPA, Riverkeeper proved that EPD was wrong. Lake Lanier was showing signs of a water body in trouble. Actions needed to be taken.

In 2008 the U.S. EPA designated Lake Lanier as "impaired," or exceeding water quality standards. As required by federal law, the state initiated a modeling project with input from stakeholders; water quality was assessed and solutions proposed. Based on this modeling and additional data collected by Riverkeeper in following years, a cleanup plan was finally approved in 2017.

The plan caps the level of nutrients that can enter the lake by requiring the tightening of wastewater permit limits and imposing management strategies on land uses in the watershed. Today, Riverkeeper staff and interns continue to monitor the lake monthly during the growing season (April–October), as they have done for the past sixteen years. Lake management decisions must be based on accurate data.

Every day, Riverkeeper works to identify potential problems, get the facts and scientific data, seek input from experts, propose solutions, and implement them with a wide variety of partners.

In the organization's second decade, Riverkeeper expanded its monitoring programs with Jason's leadership and technical skills. With donor support, we built water testing laboratories in all three of our offices. Now the organization's riverkeeper, Jason and the staff are deploying state-of-the-art devices throughout the Chattahoochee watershed to identify pollution hot spots, find the sources, and resolve problems. Science and facts matter.

CHAPTER 21

Finding the Source

December 8, 2019

A map says to you, "Read me carefully, follow me closely, doubt
me not. . . . I am the earth in the palm of your hand."
—*Beryl Markham*

I love topographic maps! They are useful and beautiful. It's easy to lose track of time while poring over these drawings that show the earth's natural and man-made features. Mountains, rivers, valleys, political boundaries, and transportation corridors.

After studying the map of the eighty-acre Cabin Creek watershed, Neill and I decide we should follow the creek and both of its perennial (continually flowing) tributaries upstream, as far as we can go on each. The map reveals that Cabin Creek rises from a place a few hundred yards above a small man-made lake not far outside the boundaries of the national park. The headwaters of one of the two tributaries is also dammed.

On a chilly, overcast morning, we walk a short distance down the well-beaten park trail and turn into the silent woods, crunching through piles of leaves—mostly oak, tulip poplar, and hickory—that release the pungent smell of late fall. Only a few hundred yards from the trail, I feel the excitement that comes with exploring a new place, seeing and experiencing things I have never seen or experienced before.

After crossing a small ridge, we descend the slope of the ravine, seeking the water that flows at its bottom. We're looking for the stream that has defined this little hardwood gorge over hundreds of years. Along the way, we pass large trees, including a pine with a skirt of emerald-green moss. It grows up the trunk in the crevasses between thick, puzzle-piece plates of bark: moss tentacles reaching upward for the life-giving water that flows down the tree when it rains.

The clouds begin to part and the temperature warms. Patches of blue sky allow sunlight to shine down through bare branches, illuminating the flowing water in Cabin Creek when we reach its banks. We walk upstream, listening to the sound of water falling over rocks on its way to the river, a sound more beautiful to my ears than a symphony. Our companions are

Cabin Creek, a tributary to the Chattahoochee River, flows through a wooded ravine of old-growth remnants. Photo: Henry Jacobs.

tiny fish, varieties of moss, ferns, and birdsong. In the foot-deep pools below small water-falls, the water is an unusual bluish green.

(The next year, I would learn that the color we observed was residue from the dyeing of the private upstream lake on Cabin Creek. The property owner told a park ranger that he didn't like the "muddy brown" color of the water, preferring an unnatural, bright turquoise instead. Because the coloring agent flowed into waters downstream of his property and into the park, EPD issued a notice of violation to the landowner. This warning may, or may not, serve as a future deterrent. I have my doubts.)

I adjust my eyes and concentrate on tree reflections in the gin-clear water that offers a mirror to the beeches, hickories, and other hardwood trees growing on the moist slopes of the ravine. Farther upstream, Neill finds a massive beech tree, surrounded by young beeches. It's 112 inches in circumference.

The best way to estimate the age of a standing tree such as this beech is to take a pencil-sized core sample. Prohibited from taking a tree core within the national park, we use a simple formula to roughly estimate the tree's age: diameter at breast height multiplied by a growth factor, which is six for beeches. The immense tree may be 210 years old. It could have been a seedling in 1813–1814, when Muscogee Creek factions and the United States fought the Creek War near the Chattahoochee River, whose name is thought to come from a Muscogee word meaning "rocks marked" or "rocks painted." The war ended when General Andrew Jackson forced the Creek Confederation to surrender more than twenty million acres of land in what is now Georgia and Alabama. In the 1820s and 1830s, the Muscogee people were forcibly removed to what is now Oklahoma.

About eight feet from the ground, the beech splits into two sturdy trunks; one of them forks again about thirty feet from the ground. On one side of its trunk, we find arborglyphs, carvings in the thin-skinned bark. A crude drawing of a hand that has widened over the years as the tree grew is obvious, as are the initials MCB. Less obvious are the other human markings.

I lay my hand with fingers spread against the cool, smooth bark, within the much larger outline of the handprint, and wonder who made this carving and how long ago. I also wonder why so many people through the ages have felt compelled to mark another living thing: the American beech tree. Carvings create rough spots that allow beech scale insects to attack the bark and sicken the tree.

I know I'll return to this beech through the seasons and over the years to admire and respect its solitary presence in this largely hidden and protected ravine, unseen by hikers who move quickly down the well-trod trail to the river.

We look upslope, beyond a fence that marks the national park boundary, and see the earthen dam that creates the private lake. The seep or spring that gives birth to Cabin Creek is somewhere on that private land.

Heading back downslope, we find a patch of bright green Boott's sedge (*Carex picta*) and a tangled mass of deadfall covered with turkey tail mushrooms (*Trametes versicolor*) in amazing colors and sizes. Turkey tails have a long history of traditional use in both Chinese and Native American natural medicine; they may even help boost immune systems and fight certain cancers. Scrambling over and around the downed trees, we eventually reach the mouth of the first tributary, the place where its waters enter Cabin Creek.

Our second upstream trek is a bit more strenuous, given the steeper slope of the ravine created by this tributary to Cabin Creek. A massive tulip popular tree's huge roots extend across the small stream to create a stair-step waterfall. Farther along, we find swampy areas with a surprising amount of sediment for the largely protected stream.

I stop to admire rock outcrops, beech roots, and ferns. It's almost more natural beauty than I can absorb until we look far upslope and see the second earthen dam that we expected from our read of the topo map. The pond created by this dam at the stream's headwaters—an amenity for another private residence—has been partially drained. Pumps and flexible pipes used to send the pond water downstream into the national park are visible on both sides of the private fence.

Huge piles of woody debris have been thrown illegally over the fence into the park. The sediment we noticed earlier may be the result of scouring from a flood of water pumped from the pond when the landowner drained it. The scene is ugly and sad. No wonder we don't find any fish in this stream.

Our hike up the second perennial tributary that enters Cabin Creek, just a quarter of a mile from the creek's confluence with the river, is breathtaking in every way. Its entire watershed is within park boundaries. It is completely protected. This unnamed stream flows through a surprisingly steep-walled ravine that is obstructed with a significant amount of deadfall and brush. We are forced to climb higher on the hill, still tracking the stream, as it becomes smaller and smaller. Finally, we reach a depression, really a damp spot, in the woods at an elevation that is nearly 150 feet above the river. We have found the tributary's source.

Several deer run across the ridge, away from us and our noisy walking, while a hawk screeches loudly and repeatedly overhead. I want to lie down on the carpet of green moss at the top of the ridge and gaze into the treetops and the sky beyond, but it's past lunchtime. We are hungry.

Our adventure is almost done, but for one last discovery—an old stone hearth covered with moss. It sits about fifteen feet from the stream in a secluded and nearly level spot, perfect for camping. It could have been last used a few decades ago or a hundred years ago. We'll never know.

While topo maps do a wonderful job of helping us visualize the earth and guiding hiking adventures like ours in the Cabin Creek watershed, another way to experience the relief and expanse of a river's watershed is to view it from the sky.

The place where a river begins, or rises, is called its source, or headwaters. It is where the tributary farthest from the river's end begins, usually just downslope of the point of highest elevation in the basin or watershed. With gravity, water moves downhill from a spring or a seep, finding its way above and below ground to an outlet at the river, and ultimately the sea. Water also flows into rivers from intermittent and ephemeral streams; they are filled primarily by rainwater and may only flow for a few hours or days.

During my riverkeeping years, I climbed into the cockpits of helicopters and small airplanes nearly a dozen times. My companions were elected officials, business leaders, photographers, and volunteer pilots with Southwings, a nonprofit that helps environmental groups conduct aerial investigations. On one occasion, I remember staring at the horizon to settle my stomach during turbulence. Most of the time, I was too engaged to feel queasy, trying to identify landmarks and contain my amazement. It was difficult to comprehend that the tiny river far below me must sustain such a massively developed region.

One of my most memorable flights was to the Chattahoochee headwaters to view a high-quality trout stream. A private landowner had illegally dredged the watercourse, rip-rapped the banks, and then built a gravel road within the protected stream buffer; she claimed incomprehensibly to be "improving" trout habitat. These egregious violations were ultimately referred by the state EPD to the U.S. Corps of Engineers. Disappointingly, the locally notorious and politically connected landowner convinced the corps representative not to enforce environmental regulations. Instead, he gave her after-the-fact permission for the illegal activities. There was nothing we could do.

We flew upstream from Atlanta, tracking the river as it flows past industrial sites, under highways, and beside endless subdivisions and shopping malls. Then, we were above the smooth, blue waters of Lake Lanier. As we reached the Chattahoochee again, upstream of the lake, the land became hillier. We could see shoals, whitewater, and tributaries plunging down slopes into the river.

Finally, we were above the national forest and the spring on the side of Coon Den Ridge, where the river begins. We had reached the farthest and highest place away from the Florida state line—where the Chattahoochee River becomes the Apalachicola River, 435 miles downstream. We couldn't see the spring from the air, but I knew it was there, its clear, cold water bubbling up from the ground, surrounded by ferns and moss.

According to geologist Bill Witherspoon, it is a curious and little-known fact that not so long ago, geologically speaking, the Upper Chattahoochee River watershed in north Georgia was about a third larger in land area. It occupied all of the mountain area south and east of the Blue Ridge Divide and a portion of western South Carolina. What caused the waters of the Chattooga and Tallulah Rivers, currently in the headwaters of the Savannah River basin, to be diverted from the Chattahoochee? A well-known geologic process called stream capture.

Also known as "river piracy" or "stream beheading," stream capture occurs when one watercourse flowing in a lower region erodes uphill and intersects the path of a stream flowing at a higher elevation. This results in the capture of all of the water that is upstream, diverting it downhill into the watershed of the capturing stream.

By the turn of the twentieth century, geologists had concluded that the Chattahoochee used to flow from the Carolina mountains along a plateau at the foot of the Blue Ridge escarpment. Below this upland, a major tributary of the faster-moving Savannah River flowed steeply through the Piedmont to the Atlantic Ocean. When the erosive reach of the headwaters of this tributary breached the Chattahoochee near the junction of the Chattooga and Tallulah Rivers, waters that were in the upper portion of the Chattahoochee were diverted into the basin of the Savannah.

More recently, geologists and map enthusiasts have noted that a head branch of the Oconee River lies within a mile of the Chattahoochee near Gainesville, Georgia, where it is eroding the side of the higher elevation Chattahoochee. In geologic time, it is highly likely that the Chattahoochee will again be "beheaded" by these erosive processes. Its headwaters will then flow downstream into the Oconee and Altamaha Rivers before spilling into the Atlantic Ocean.

Earth's history tells us that nothing is permanent.

CHAPTER 22
A Tonic for Windowless Rooms

December 18, 2019

On a cold, mid-December day, with Randy in tow, I walk into the national park to again bear witness to nature's cycles along the Cabin Creek trail. The shiny green leaves of laurel, holly, doghobble, and southern magnolia contrast with the copper-colored leaves still dangling from beech branches. The silvery bigleaf magnolia leaves still litter the forest floor, but they are beginning to curl and crumble, finally starting the decomposition process with the help of microbes that will eventually turn them into soil.

The creek and its tributaries are full of water, talking loudly in a language that I can sense but not fully understand. The river is high, jabbering noisily on its way to the sea, hundreds of miles downstream. When Randy and I reach the bamboo forest, the strong wind is knocking the tall shoots against each other. The percussive sounds add rhythm to the water music in my ears.

We walk through the giant grass stems to the riverbank, where two magnificent sycamore trees lean gracefully over the water, their branches waving in the wind. Criss-crossing the ground beneath them are the vigorous surface roots that are typical of these natives. I see that two large roots, one from each sycamore, appear to have grown together, creating a strong anchor and an enlarged circulatory system for the towering trees. I may have found an example of a natural process called "inosculation," from the Latin *osculare*, "to kiss."

Considered uncommon, the inosculation process usually starts when tree roots, branches, or even trunks, typically of the same species, come into contact with each other. Over time, as they rub together from natural movement, bark wears away and exposes the cambium cell layer (living tissue) of the roots. When trees are compatible, the cambium layers fuse together, instead of continuing to brush against each other when the wind blows. Eventually, the tree heals at the junction and forms bark over the fused cells. Stronger together, the two trees become one, sharing the same lifeblood.

My first clear memory of sycamores is of those that majestically line the Chattahoochee between Atlanta and West Point Lake. This is the place where I came to love their massive trunks and open crowns with huge, crooked branches: pure white in the upper portion of older trees where the bark has sloughed off. The seventy-mile section of river downstream of Atlanta is my favorite.

About an hour southwest of Atlanta, there is a stretch of the Chattahoochee that is largely unknown. It divides two counties and then flows through a third before emptying into West Point Lake. There are no bridges, few riverside structures other than a power plant, and little evidence of the big city some fifty miles upstream.

Seeking nature and adventure, my younger son, Robert, and I slipped into kayaks at McIntosh Reserve Park in Carroll County on a warm October morning in the early 2000s. Our group consisted of a dozen paddlers, eager to spend some river time in this less-traveled section of the Chattahoochee. We would camp overnight on her shores.

Almost immediately, I could feel the tension falling from my shoulders and into the moving water that surrounded my boat. I'm not sure which parts of the trip spoke to me most eloquently—the bald eagle that flew over our heads and led us downriver, the musical sound of water running over rocks at Bush Head Shoals, the bright sweetgum, sycamore, and maple leaves decorating the water's surface, or the sight of my son happily surfing the shoals in his kayak.

It was the tonic I desperately needed, after too many long meetings in windowless rooms with stale air and harsh fluorescent lights. I wished that more of the people who make consequential decisions about the river's future would join me on the water. A few did over the years, but not nearly enough.

A personal experience with the Chattahoochee can be transforming, educational at the very least. Perhaps then, major decisions about the river would be based on all of the values that the Chattahoochee River has to offer—not just its utility as a key ingredient for economic growth at nearly any cost.

CHAPTER 23

Not for the Faint of Heart

January 8, 2020

What a beautiful, bright, blue-sky day! The open winter landscape reigns, and I feel as though I can see every single tree in the forest, each standing on a leafy carpet. I don't miss the showy green spring foliage that will alter this winter view in just a few months, though that new growth will be a joy when it arrives. I love the seasons for the wondrous variety of experiences that each has to offer.

With plant leaves and stems no longer in the way, I can finally scramble down a steep slope beside the trail. I want to explore the bottom of the deep Cabin Creek ravine, not far from the stream's confluence with the river. In the little gorge, I find a small spring, emerald-colored moss, mature beech trees, thickets of dark green doghobble, and interesting designs in the bark of a fallen tree.

Leaf-shorn trees backed by the blue sky are clearly reflected in the flowing stream. I want to plunge my hands into the cold water to see if I can touch them. At the river, I walk beside the water all the way to the bamboo forest. I run my hands over the smooth, sturdy green stems. So many sensory experiences on this winter day!

Walking back uphill, I spy a large beech along Cabin Creek with a huge, natural hollow. A young beech is rising from one of the visible roots in its shallow, spreading root system. Being shade tolerant, it's not unusual for a beech tree to sprout under its parent from an adventitious bud in a surface root, then reach for the canopy and sunlight.

As they age, beech trees often become hollow at the base, providing shelter for animals—and even people, should they need the refuge. I can imagine crawling inside this beech hollow for safety if a storm ever surprises me on one of my walks. My hope is that I'll be able to scramble up and down forested slopes and riverbanks and tuck into tree hollows for years to come, albeit a bit more slowly and carefully.

Riverkeeping can require a great deal of physical scrambling and maneuvering. In and out of boats and the water, up and down boulders and steep slopes, across pipelines and logs. Finding ways to safely and legally access industrial and construction sites and other potential threats to the river.

One of my most memorable scrambles was a hike in the late 1990s down the middle of the Chattahoochee, about a dozen miles downstream of Chattahoochee Gap and the mountain spring that gives birth to the river in north Georgia. On a warm day in midsummer, our small group set off on a trip described by our leader, Joe Cook, as "not for the faint of heart." Six miles and seven hours after embarking on our wet and slippery hike, we finished exhausted, damp, and dirty. We had safely navigated the water and a spectacular landscape with no broken bones, just a few scrapes and bruises.

The Chattahoochee is about fifteen feet wide and very shallow in its upper reaches within the Chattahoochee National Forest, where we began our walk near a primitive campground. Given the extremely steep and rocky slopes, thick with vegetation on each side of the river, we were forced to stay in the water for all but the last mile of our trek, when we found an old railroad bed along the river that was passable.

Initially, we walked gingerly, trying to keep our feet dry by stepping on stones. It soon became obvious that boldly walking through the water with some rock-hopping was the only way to make any real progress.

Shin-deep in the cold water, we could feel the river's strength and see water-sculpted boulders and smooth riverbed stones in shades of orange and brown. Waterfalls cascaded over slick, black rocks beneath cantilevered rhododendron bushes. Small tributaries plunged into deep pools in the river with oxygenating bubbles—the lungs of aquatic life, all life. It was pure magic: the mystery of water and plants and life.

Crane-fly orchid (*Tipularia discolor*), a perennial woodland orchid, produces a single leaf in the fall with a striking purple underside. A flower stem appears in midsummer with features similar to the stilt-like legs, slender body, and wings of a crane fly. Photo: Don Hunter.

CHAPTER 24

Does Anyone Own Water?

February 2, 2020

Earth provides enough to satisfy every man's needs,
but not every man's greed.
—*Mahatma Gandhi*

There are more people on the trail this beautiful Sunday afternoon than I have ever seen. Neill joins me for today's walk. The thin, pale brown beech leaves flutter in the breeze, sounding like wind chimes as they shake against each other. For the umpteenth time, I tell Neill how much I love them and wonder how I've missed their winter beauty my whole life, until now. He patiently listens, used to my repetitions regarding the things I love.

A few hundred yards down the trail, I notice a warty-looking burl on the trunk of a small tree. Usually appearing as a rounded, woody outgrowth covered with bark, a burl is made up of a collection of tree cells called callus tissue. This tissue grows faster than regular tree cells and typically fills with undeveloped buds. A stress, such as an injury from storm damage or disease, can cause the burl formation as a wound response, an attempt to protect the tree. Woodworkers love burls because of their unique ring patterns and abstract designs within the wood grain.

At the bottom of the creek's ravine, bigleaf magnolia leaves remain visible—still slowly decomposing more than four months after they have fallen. Tiny organisms are turning the huge leaves into delicate lace with veins that once supported the vanishing gossamer organic matter.

We meet Georgia Tech students from the school's trailblazer club with rock climbing equipment and bouldering pads; they're headed to the rocky palisade at the river. A young woman is walking her dog, Banjo. She works at the Chattahoochee Nature Center and shows us several interesting plants, including the perennial crane-fly orchid (*Tipularia discolor*), which grows in moist, humus-rich soils near streams in deciduous forests.

Emerging in late fall and visible through the winter, each single, green crane-fly leaf—often found with spots and bumps on its surface—has an unexpected, bright purple underside.

145

The leaves disappear by late spring to early summer. A few months later, a stem of fifteen to twenty inches with tiny, delicate blossoms will appear in the place where the leaf grew.

As though a veil has been lifted from my eyes, I now see these unassuming woodland orchid leaves everywhere along the path, peeking out from the piles of brown leaves that protect and nourish them. The invisible has suddenly been made visible!

Neill sits, reading, on the steps of the old cabin near the confluence of Cabin Creek and the river while I pick up microtrash along the shoreline. I think about how relaxed I am whenever I'm in this peaceful place that changes almost daily through the seasons—yet also stays the same.

The low river drifts downstream: the liquid treasure that people have fought over for centuries around the world. As the earth warms and water sources vanish from places where they were once abundant, these battles will multiply.

High water, low water. Who loses and who wins, when a river is low and decisions must be made to allocate limited water supplies among various users? Does water "belong" to anyone? Can it be fairly and equitably shared? If so, who makes and who enforces those decisions? How much water do rivers need to function as they have for millennia, providing habitat and sustenance for fish, amphibians, reptiles, birds, insects, mammals, and humans?

The answers to such questions are critical for communities along the Chattahoochee River and all of the planet's waterways. Exacerbated by the climate crisis, water insecurity is one of the greatest threats facing populations around the world. Uncertain and erratic water supplies could cost some regions up to 6 percent of their gross domestic product, spur migration, and spark conflict, according to the World Bank.

More frequent droughts in the Southeast were noted beginning in the 1980s and 1990s, leading to greater demands for water from downstream states for their users. Some elected officials and bureaucrats in Georgia, along with the experts they engaged, decided to promote a concept new to our state: markets to allocate and manage water as a commodity.

Explained simply, water would be sold to the highest bidder through water permit trading, a practice similar to that of water-use and allocation laws employed in arid western states. Using this approach, water would no longer belong to the public, regulated by the state government for everyone's benefit. It would belong to whoever could get a withdrawal permit.

These permits could be sold. The water could be piped from poorer parts of the state to the wealthier Atlanta region, or even out of state. Those unable to compete financially for larger marketable volumes of water—smaller communities and businesses, family farms, and, of course, water-dependent plant and animal life—would eventually lose out in such a market-based system.

Four nonprofit environmental organizations founded the Georgia Water Coalition in 2002 to stop the attempted transformation of Georgia's water into a marketable commodity—allocated not according to need or plan but to the agreements between willing buyers and sellers seeking profits. The coalition's mission is to ensure that the state's waters will always be considered a shared, public resource under the law, managed in the public interest and not available for private sale.

Riverkeeper was one of the four nonprofits approached by Phyllis Bowen, the strategic director of the Georgia-based Sapelo Foundation. She urged us to develop a broad coalition to counter this attempted water grab by speculators with money and political clout. We were galvanized by the realization of how fundamentally the permit trading proposal would affect the future of water availability and river health in Georgia for generations.

The Charles Stewart Mott Foundation also helped finance the coalition's work to ensure sufficient volumes of flow in Georgia rivers to support healthy ecosystems and communities. Over twenty years, Mott provided $35 million to fifty organizations working to protect the biologically diverse freshwater systems in six southeastern states. Foundation staff realized that our rivers, streams, and lakes were not adequately protected by existing laws or regulatory agencies and that local environmental groups needed support from national funders.

An independent consultant hired by Mott to assess its decades of investment concluded: "The Georgia Water Coalition is an exceptional leader on critically important water issues within the state of Georgia and the southeastern region. In a time of divisiveness and political polarization, the Coalition stands as an example of how people with different backgrounds and viewpoints can agree and work together on shared concerns."

When the coalition was created in the early 2000s, Georgia's conservation groups did not work closely together on issues and rarely shared funding for projects; there was too much competition and a reluctance to do the difficult work to reach agreement. Organizing and managing the coalition were not easy tasks, especially in the early years. It took time and patience to get used to each other's different styles and find common ground.

My friend and mentor Jerry McCollum—then director of the Georgia Wildlife Federation and one of the coalition's cofounders—was instrumental in bringing us together and keeping us on task. John Sibley of the Georgia Conservancy, another stellar environmental leader, played a significant role in the coalition's successes. Winning a major victory together near midnight on April 25, 2003, was the motivation we needed to cement our working relationships, which continue to this day.

I remember the hallways of the Georgia state capitol being frantic that night in 2003, near the completion of what was then the longest session of the Georgia legislature since the 1880s. Thirty minutes before the end of the session, the much-debated question of who would determine how Georgia manages its rivers, lakes, estuaries, and aquifers remained undecided.

H.B. 237, the bill introduced that year to create a state water plan, had been the subject of more than a dozen conference committee meetings, in which House and Senate members attempted to resolve their differences in the legislation. The most controversial issue was whether or not the state's waterways would continue to be managed as a public resource or become a commodity that could be sold to the highest bidder through permit trading.

State senators who opposed the commodity approach planned to talk the bill to death, making speeches until midnight, the mandated end of the session, meaning the measure would die on the senate floor, when that body adjourned sine die, leaving no more days for further action. The odds that our coalition and local government allies would prevail against the powerful interests that supported using a market approach to manage water were slim. Led by the Georgia Chamber of Commerce, major industries and large private water users, along with their lobbyists, had dominated the water debate.

The head of the state chamber at the time was George Israel: a man described as "unabashedly pro-growth," who believed that environmentalists were "burdening" business. As he told *Georgia Trend* magazine in 2003, "We're competing with China and other places that do things differently. We can sit here with our clean laws—our clean air and water stuff—to the extent we cannot compete in the world."

More enlightened local business leaders, such as Roy Richards with Southwire (one of North America's largest wire and cable producers) and Ray Anderson with Interface (a global leader in modular flooring), had a different view. They understood that a clean, healthy environment contributes to economic growth and that water must be treated as a common shared public resource.

At 11:36 p.m., a shout came from the House side of the state capitol, and then the news. In two successive votes, the House had overwhelmingly rejected the inequitable marketing approach to manage Georgia's waters. Silence in the halls turned to jubilation as coalition members from around the state and supporting representatives of local governments, crucial to the victory, literally jumped for joy. The post–sine die celebration party at a local tavern was legendary.

H.B. 237 returned and passed the legislature the following year, mandating Georgia's first water management plan. The language that would have dramatically and inequitably changed the way water has been allocated in Georgia for hundreds of years was gone.

It has been said that a river cuts through rock not because of power but because of its persistence. Our sweet victory at the capitol underscored the importance of collaboration and dogged persistence.

CHAPTER 25

Trash—and Dead Goats

February 16, 2020

It is a chilly, gray day, following a week of storms. A red-tailed hawk sits on a tree branch above the parking area, watching the curious humans admire it from below. The leaves on the ground near the trail to the river have been pushed aside by torrents of flowing water, creating new, but short-lived, streams heading downslope. Water moves endlessly downhill, always seeking the sea. Following the heavy rain, the bigleaf magnolia leaves have finally merged into the leaf litter and are no longer dominant.

The young beech trees are even more glorious under the winter sky, with leaf colors ranging from old parchment and tan to gold. Today their outstretched branches look like arms held high in triumph. The large, older beeches remind me of elephants with their smooth, light gray, and occasionally wrinkled bark. Their exposed, chunky roots look like elephant legs that are propping up the straight trunks. Some beech tree roots stretch across the ground like tentacles, gripping steep slopes, large rocks, and streambanks.

The river is high and the water is slate-gray with purplish hues and white waves. No rocks are visible in the torrent, which was clearly well over riverbanks earlier. A wrack line of small pieces of trash meanders from a few feet to about ten feet from the riverbank. Puzzle pieces of Styrofoam in all shapes and sizes mark the distance that the water reached. Vines and other plants along the shore wear floating debris.

I fill two trash bags with Styrofoam, straws, decades-old pop tops, tennis balls, a large blue plastic container of antifreeze, a shoe insert, a glove, plastic cups, plastic bottles, plastic container tops, pens, a Glade spray can, cigarette holders, cellophane, and plastic wrapping.

Everywhere I look, there are indications of an early spring: tiny green shoots, new leaves, red buds on branches, hepatica still blooming, and yellow halberd-leaved violets (*Viola hastata*). A nut lies on a rock, cracked open to its bright red innards by some small animal. Single purple-bottomed *Tipularia* leaves that will disappear in a few months before the flowers bloom next summer still line the trail to the river.

As I walk back to the parking area along the gravel access road, I spot a bright green object decorating the bare branches of a small tree. Someone has tied a plastic bag containing dog waste onto the limb, about five feet off the ground.

Why go to so much trouble? People! How hard is it to carry the plastic bag to the trash can in the parking area? I remove it and put it in my bag, yet again amazed and disturbed at the failure of too many people to respect the public lands that belong to all of us.

Trash can be a galvanizing topic for many people, especially river and nature lovers. We are disgusted at the sight of Styrofoam, plastic bags, plastic bottles, and balls of every sort that float in the water, moving from one riverbank to another on their voyages downriver.

Most of this debris arrives in the river via tributaries, which serve as natural conduits for storm drains that collect rainwater and trash from streets, parking lots, yards, and commercial and industrial sites. Some trash is thrown directly into rivers, usually off bridges—the out of sight, out of mind attitude that has historically been the way people dealt with something they didn't want. Old furniture, appliances, tires (oh, so many tires . . .), mattresses, toys, and clothes.

One of the strangest trash-related phone calls I ever received came, in the late 1990s, from an employee at Georgia Power's Plant Mc-Donough-Atkinson on the Chattahoochee, immediately downstream of the city. She asked, rather matter-of-factly, if Riverkeeper would please remove a rotting goat from the river. It had gotten stuck in an eddy (an area of swirling water) in front of the plant's water intake grate. Plant workers refused to make needed repairs to the intake until the goat and the nauseating smell emanating from the carcass were gone. I responded that our organization did not manage such waste and suggested that she call the local animal services agency.

In the years since I retired, Riverkeeper has regularly found more goats (and chickens)—at least five hundred and all headless—in the same area of the Chattahoochee. These animals may have been sacrificed as part of Afro-Caribbean religious rituals, possibly to safeguard the journeys of drug smugglers. In late summer 2022, headless goats and chicken carcasses were found far upstream on land near the river within the Chatta-hoochee River National Recreation Area. Collaborating with the media and various enforcement agencies, Riverkeeper is working to identify the perpetrators and put an end to the dumping of the carcasses.

On a warm January afternoon in the mid-2000s, I took my kayak to the river in the national park to conduct a one-person cleanup. Paddling to some strainers—the downed tree branches and other debris that catch trash—I found, among the usual detritus, a large plastic trash bag that was wedged behind a log. It was filled with something heavy, as the bag was floating low in the water. I touched it with my finger. The contents of the bag felt pliable, soft—and strange.

When I tried to dislodge the bag, it started to float away, so I paddled closer. Looking inside a small hole, I saw brown fur. Someone had evidently put a dead dog, possibly a family pet, in the plastic bag and thrown it in the river. Not wanting to leave it in the water, I pushed the heavy bag toward the shore. After many clumsy maneuvers, I was able to get it onto the beach, where a park visitor helped me pull the bag out of the water. Rangers handled the proper disposal of the dead animal.

A few weeks later, I walked the park trail near the place I had found the dead dog, trying to find solace in nature, after being told it was time to put down our fourteen-year-old family dog. A mix between a Labrador retriever, Great Dane, and a few other breeds, Molly B. was my first and only dog, although I've since been blessed with granddogs. She helped me through a divorce, the departures of my sons to northern colleges, and so much more.

On that cold, gloomy February day, as I walked beside the river heartbroken, I found some comfort from my sorrow in the brisk air, the flowing water, the bare branches of the winter trees bending in the wind—and in the continuity of life.

After Riverkeeper filed its lawsuit against the city of Atlanta for chronic sewage overflows, reporters and their photographers would ask us to take them to a polluted creek or for a boat ride on the river so they could "see" pollution. This was not an easy task, since bacteria, chemicals, and other toxins are typically invisible to the human eye.

My go-to place to satisfy their requests was Clear Creek, then an inappropriately named stream. It runs next to a small shopping center on the edge of my neighborhood in midtown Atlanta. Before the city upgraded its sewer system, I could always count on this creek to provide trash-filled visuals to satisfy the photographers, especially after a heavy rain. Items found in toilets ended up hanging from the branches of small shrubs and trees growing near the water.

One memorable trip with a photographer for a national newspaper yielded the most astounding sight of all. He wanted to see where the city's largest sewage treatment plant discharges directly into the Chattahoochee. We drove to a parking area near the R. M. Clayton plant and walked to a platform above the frothy, chlorine-smelling water; it was flowing out of a massive pipe into the river. As we looked around us, we saw that every tree was covered with condoms: thousands of them swayed in the poststorm breeze.

Things that people thought they had gotten rid of with a flush had again seen the light of day. The sewage plant had apparently malfunctioned and disgorged all it held without any treatment. Such was the state of Atlanta's sewer system in the 1990s and early 2000s.

In 2011 Riverkeeper, Upper Chattahoochee Chapter of Trout Unlimited, National Park Service, and other partners organized the inaugural Sweep the Hooch Cleanup at a dozen sites within the Chattahoochee River National Recreation Area. Today, the annual event engages more than a thousand volunteers, including fifty organizations and government agencies. Paddlers, waders, and walkers work together to sweep the Chattahoochee clean along a one-hundred-mile section of the river.

Seeking new ways to achieve a trash-free Chattahoochee, Riverkeeper is now installing small instream trash collection devices into tributaries to the river. Floating booms guide trash into wire-mesh containers that can be emptied after a rainstorm. Results are promising.

During Riverkeeper's first twenty-five years, we removed at least two million pounds of trash and tires from the Chattahoochee, its tributaries, and its lakes with the help of thousands of volunteers—enough to fill twenty-five eighteen-wheel trucks. A significant portion of the two million pounds was pulled out of tributaries to the river pursuant to the consent decree that settled our lawsuit against the city of Atlanta.

For a year in the late 1990s, a team of workers hired by the city removed everything larger than a cigarette butt from thirty-seven miles of streams. I still remember walking down Proctor Creek with Tyler Richards, then the city's environmental compliance manager, to view a section that had been cleaned of trash. It looked like a pristine mountain stream that had been relocated to the middle of the city.

We drove on to a still-trashed section of the same creek, which was disgusting. It was filled with broken toilets, bedsprings, plastic, and the ubiquitous tires. Around a bend in the waterway, we could see dozens of orange-clad workers moving toward us like a human vacuum cleaner. They rolled tires and carried trash bags and large metal objects. I felt a lump in my throat, watching these people toil to help bring our city streams back to light and life.

Later that day, I stood on a road bridge over Proctor Creek in northwest Atlanta and watched six old cars, some from the 1970s, being hauled out of the stream. Neighbors said they had tried for decades to get the city to remove the vehicles and trash. They were thrilled to finally have their creek back.

By the end of the cleanup project, the city had spent $5 million to remove and appropriately dispose of 568 tons of trash and debris from the streams flowing through intown neighborhoods. This massive cleanup was the most visible and immediately gratifying result of our lawsuit. It would be many years before the entire sewer system could be repaired and the quality of water in city streams and in the river downstream of Atlanta dramatically improved.

Despite our efforts, and those of many others through the years, the river continues to serve as a dumping ground for too many of the things that people no longer want—be they dead animals, tires, or appliances. Often, it seems, garbage attracts more garbage.

It's not just the visible trash that harms our waters, wildlife, and ourselves. Microplastics—less than 0.2 inches long—have increasingly been found in waterways (including the Chattahoochee), the air, and even human blood around the world. These tiny pieces of plastic debris result from the breakdown of consumer products (synthetic textiles, tires, and personal care products) and from industrial processes. We live in what's been called a "soup of plastic," derived from fossil fuels. Testing protocols, technologies, and other solutions to remove microplastics from the environment are just beginning to emerge.

Aldo Leopold wrote in *A Sand County Almanac*: "We abuse land because we regard it as a commodity belonging to us. When we see land as a community to which we belong, we may begin to use it with love and respect."

Teach the children.

A river birch (*Betula nigra*) and an American sycamore (*Platanus occidentalis*), both water-loving trees, grow on a small island in the Chattahoochee River. Photo: Henry Jacobs.

CHAPTER 26

Ballfields versus Ancient Trees

March 8, 2020

Deep down, at the molecular heart of life, the trees and
we are essentially identical.

—Carl Sagan

I'm getting over a bad head cold, but I want to see spring begin to emerge along Cabin Creek, so I head to the woods and the river. It's a beautiful day in the upper fifties. I spot a few trillium plants along the trail and colonies of yellow, halberd-leaved violets.

Star chickweed (*Stellaria pubera*), another spring ephemeral that I find in bloom, is used medicinally for a variety of health conditions: stomach and bowel problems, blood disorders, asthma and other lung diseases, scurvy, and various skin conditions. One small lavender hepatica bloom remains.

The most exciting find on this walk is what appears to be a family of beech trees. A large beech trunk lies on the ground with three branches or shoots rising high into the forest canopy from its seemingly dead body. It's not unusual for a fallen tree to sprout new stems from adventitious buds on its trunk that reach for the sun, straining to continue the tree's life through regeneration. A few yards away from the fallen beech and the sprouts I consider its offspring stands a large, healthy beech.

In my decades of hiking through woods and over mountains, I have never seen a tree grouping quite like this one. I can't wait to examine it in more detail on another visit. How is it possible that I've walked this trail for the past ten months and never noticed these trees?

The beech leaves are finally done until next winter. Some still tremble in the breeze, but they are shriveling, no longer as luminescent as new parchment paper. For the second time, I cannot find the little fish in the bend of the creek. Did they finally swim downstream to bigger waters? Small, bright green patches are emerging from the leaf litter on the north-facing slope where the fly poison plants grow. A woman and young boy picnic on a large, rectangular rock in Cabin Creek. People and dogs fill the trail and woods today.

The river is bank full, the highest level I've seen since last spring. The Corps of Engineers must be releasing a large volume of water from Buford Dam to lower Lake Lanier. The reservoir is five feet above its normal pool from winter rains—a dramatic difference from the previous summer's drought.

The small sycamore tree and a river birch that stand as sentinels on a tiny island just offshore have water up to their shins today; their island is submerged. Over the past year, these water-loving trees and the slip of land on which they grow have served as my barometer for the river's moods. They help me gauge her depth and speed, her complexion, and her temper.

Polypody ferns (*Polypodium virginianum*) are emerging on fallen logs. Pale green fiddleheads are beginning to unfurl between the decaying fronds of last year's Christmas ferns. Spring is almost here!

Every spring, rare pink lady's slipper orchids (*Cypripedium acaule*) bloom near ancient white oak trees and a small stream in a nature preserve on the southside of metro Atlanta; the land lies within the city of East Point. Once part of a plantation, the property was owned by generations of a single family for nearly two centuries, beginning in the early 1800s—until it was deeded to East Point.

Historians and forest experts believe the unusual stand of old oaks, one of which is estimated to be two hundred years old, may have been planted as shade trees on the plantation. An urban forester with the U.S. Forest Service was quoted in an *Atlanta Journal-Constitution* article, saying: "I don't think you will find a stand of white oaks like that, at least I can't think of one that comes to mind. Stands like that are around, but they are very uncommon."

Oaks, notably white oaks, support more wild creatures—from butterflies to bears—than any other tree in North America; they are a keystone tree species. During their lifetimes, oak trees are estimated to drop as many as three million acorns. Blue jays, which are heavily dependent on oaks, may bury for later use, if they can find them, as many as 4,500 acorns each fall, helping spread these mighty trees across the landscape.

Today, the white oaks in East Point are massive guardians in the midst of twenty-seven acres of land that have been permanently protected. It took a village of local officials, neighbors, reporters, nonprofits, and foundations to save the forest.

When this property was granted to East Point, the city considered clear-cutting the woods to build ball fields but decided to sell the land to the Fulton County Board of Education in 1999; the board developed plans to build a new elementary school. Construction of the new school would require cutting most of the white oaks, piping a portion of the small stream, and extensively grading the long-undisturbed soils in the old forest.

Too often, government officials decide to build public facilities on marginal land they already own—no matter its condition, the impacts, or potential for other uses, such as public green space. Natural areas that could serve as learning laboratories end up being destroyed to save money in the short term while environmental benefits to the community are lost forever. Clean water is one of those benefits.

Neighbors who loved the forest with the old oaks organized to fight the school proposal. They sought the assistance of local nonprofits with expertise in protecting trees (Trees Atlanta), land (Green South Fulton), and streams (Riverkeeper). Our groups were joined by the Conservation Fund, a well-known national organization capable of raising funds to purchase the property, if the board of education agreed to sell. Several local foundations also supported the project.

Riverkeeper became involved because the stream to be piped flows into a major tributary to the Chattahoochee. The health of the river depends on the condition of these streams—just like our hearts are dependent on healthy arteries, veins, and capillaries. We hoped to keep this stream in good health.

Georgia law requires the protection of natural, vegetated buffers of twenty-five feet along both banks of warmwater (nontrout) streams, unless the state issues a variance; under certain circumstances, such as hardship cases, variances can be provided when a developer has no alternative but to harm the buffer to achieve reasonable project goals. Without following its own rules, the Georgia Environmental Protection Division gave the county a variance to pipe the stream to build the school.

Riverkeeper filed a legal appeal, noting that the county had other places where it could build a school. In other words, there were alternatives that didn't require harming the stream. The court found the organization's arguments to be persuasive and overturned the state's variance.

In the meantime, media coverage and political pressure to save the forest from bulldozers had increased significantly. After extensive (and often difficult) negotiations, the board of education finally agreed to give up the property and build their new school on another site.

Once East Point reclaimed the property, the city granted a conservation easement to a nonprofit land trust associated with Riverkeeper to permanently protect the forest from any development. The park was officially named for the family who had owned the land since the 1800s: the Connally family.

In the ensuing years, Riverkeeper worked with the city to stop sewer overflows in the park, plant native vegetation, and remove tons of trash. I remember the satisfaction of carrying part of a broken toilet out of the woods during a cleanup event on a cold winter day. With a new Weed Wrench in hand, Neill was thrilled at the speed with which he could uproot invasive bushes and exhausted himself in an hour.

Today, volunteers maintain a narrow trail through the forest. They plant native shrubs and trees. They're also slowly removing the nonnative English ivy that covers much of the forest floor.

On a warm summer morning, with cicadas buzzing in the treetops, Neill and I visited the park for the first time in half a dozen years. There were small red flags where the lady's slippers had bloomed a few months earlier. "Hank Aaron"—the largest of the white oaks, named for the Atlanta-based Major League Baseball star—still reaches for the sky. The tree is more than 110 feet tall with a trunk circumference of at least sixteen feet. There was no trash anywhere in the park. A handful of people walked dogs and talked quietly as they enjoyed the shady urban sanctuary.

CHAPTER 27
Truth, Justice, and Reconciliation

March 15, 2020

Hopelessness is the enemy of justice.
—*Bryan Stevenson*

As Neill and I begin our walk down the Cabin Creek trail, the weather is pleasant, but clouds and cooler temperatures soon follow. I'm anxious to show him the fallen beech tree and her offspring. Forest ecologists would consider this dead (or dying) beech and her sprouts to be one tree: one individual surviving through regeneration. I continue to think of them as a family.

The offspring have become sturdy forest sentinels growing a few feet apart, ramrod straight, reaching for the sun with their mother tree as their foundation. They were sustained by her decaying body in their early decades as they developed their own roots. Firmly embedded in the forest floor, they now reach around her trunk in an embrace.

Once the fallen tree has completely decomposed and become soil, stilt-like roots that support the trunks of her offspring may frame voids where she once lay: emptiness that reveals the past, if our eyes can see it. As often occurs in human families, one of the beech offspring has had advantages. A larger opening in the tree canopy has provided more sunlight to nourish faster growth in the biggest sprout.

We've brought a tape measure to record tree circumferences of this family group so we can estimate the approximate age of each member using the formula published by the International Society of Arboriculture. Based on the fallen tree's measurement, I determine she was nearly seventy-five years old when she fell. Her strongest offspring, who has had the advantage of more sun, is about sixty years old. Their approximate, combined age of 135 years indicates that the fallen tree could have begun growing in the 1880s.

In retirement, I've been researching my family history—learning about my own roots, which originated in England, Scotland, Ireland, and Germany's Rhineland. After crossing the Atlantic Ocean in the early 1600s and mid-1700s, my ancestors settled in the forests and on the farmland of Connecticut, Virginia, and Pennsylvania. My grandparents, born in the 1870s and 1880s, were very likely children when this mother beech began her life in the damp

Three healthy sprouts from a fallen American beech (*Fagus grandifolia*) in Cabin Creek ravine reveal the tree's attempt to regenerate. Photo: Henry Jacobs.

ravine along Cabin Creek. She fell, I estimate, in the late 1950s, just a few years after my parents, my sister, Cathy, and I moved from Virginia to Georgia.

I like thinking about my human family's connection through time to this tree family and the historical events that occurred while the beech trees grew in the rich soil and humid ravine of Cabin Creek and Cathy and I grew beside the little stream and wooded hill in the city. Like the beech tree sprouts, we also carry our ancestors' genetic material into our own uncertain futures.

On weekends in the 2000s, Neill and I often explored tributaries to the Chattahoochee that flow through the less-traveled sections of its urban watershed. Industrial parks, junkyards, abandoned neighborhoods, construction sites, landfills, kudzu woods, and land near railroad lines and under highway bridges.

In these places, we found unexpected natural beauty, along with heartbreaking volumes of trash and pollution. Not far from one creek we discovered in northwest Atlanta, we found remnants of a dark story from the city's post–Civil War history—one that, like so many others, was never taught in our southern schools.

The stream in the area we investigated, then unnamed on maps, flows behind an old landfill and an auto dump on a long-blighted road formerly known as Bankhead Highway. In recognition of a legendary civil rights attorney, the road is now called Donald Lee Hollowell Parkway. A multifamily housing project and an elementary school were located immediately upstream. The waters of this creek merge with Proctor Creek, then flow another half-mile or so before entering the Chattahoochee River.

At the confluence of Proctor Creek and the river lies a seventy-five-acre tract of land that was owned by Chattahoochee Brick Company for a century beginning in the 1870s. Its founder was former Atlanta mayor and Confederate captain James English. Here, convict laborers—nearly all Black and many jailed for petty crimes—from local penitentiaries were exploited, horribly abused, and forced to live in filthy conditions. Some died in what has been called a "death camp."

The gruesome history came to light in Douglas Blackmon's Pulitzer

Prize–winning book, *Slavery by Another Name* (2008). Blackmon reported that at the turn of the twentieth century—decades after slavery was ostensibly abolished—the brick company leased the labor of convicts from the state to produce millions of handmade bricks; they were used for city streets, sidewalks, cemeteries, and other purposes. It is believed that makeshift graves were created on site, and likely remain.

Civil rights leaders, neighbors, and environmental activists protested a fuel terminal initially proposed for this site in 2017. They hoped to memorialize the people who suffered there by preserving the property as permanent green space, at once protecting the river from industrial pollution. In 2022 the Atlanta City Council acquired the property for $22 million with assistance from the Conservation Fund to create the long-advocated park and memorial. The site's past will be preserved and interpreted with historical exhibits.

Bryan Stevenson—widely acclaimed public interest lawyer and founder of the Equal Justice Initiative—has said: "We need an era of truth and justice in this country; we need to have truth and reconciliation. . . . There's something better waiting for us that we can't get to until we have the courage to talk honestly about our past."

What happened at Chattahoochee Brick is an important part of Atlanta's past. The city's action to invest in its preservation and memorialize its tragic story is a beginning.

When Neill and I explored the mature, diverse forest of approximately thirty acres that surrounds the creek near the landfill in the early 2000s, we were not aware of the nearby brickworks and its sad history. Although the area we discovered was full of trash and the waterways were obviously polluted, this pocket of nature was also beautiful and surprising for its size in such a highly urbanized setting.

A tiny stream flowing beside the old landfill was bright orange with what appeared to be leachate (contaminated liquid); it had a strong chemical odor. The larger, unnamed creek, which was crossed multiple times by a massive sewer pipe with brick manhole columns, contained white strands and clumps of bacteria, the classic sign of chronic pollution. Could the columns, which wore their covers like jaunty hats, have been made at Chattahoochee Brick, I now wonder?

When it rained, the sewer pipe was unable to contain the volume and pressure of the contaminated water that rushed through it, resulting in the askew manhole lids and sewage overflows into the creek and forest. Hundreds of tires, construction debris, mounds of asphalt, and more poked out from behind the trees and dense vegetation.

With multiple problems and pollution sources, this creek presented a considerable challenge. Our first step was to contact Browning Ferris Industries, Inc., then the owner of the landfill, to discuss the potentially toxic leachate flowing into the smaller stream on their site. The company agreed to work with us to repair breaches in the landfill, remove trash, and stabilize the streambank. We discussed the sewage overflows with Atlanta officials, told them we'd seen children playing near the water, and urged them to make this stream a priority. The city was beginning to overhaul the entire sewer system as a requirement of the consent decree that settled Riverkeeper's lawsuit against the city.

With the help of Na'Taki Osborne Jelks and Darryl Haddock—leaders of West Atlanta Watershed Alliance—we involved neighbors with our project. On a beautiful late fall day that I vividly remember, we worked together to collect a ton of trash: residents, high school and university students, businesses, and Browning Ferris employees. We rolled more than eighty tires out of the area, pushing and pulling them over rocks and fallen trees.

Given all the love and attention the stream was receiving, we decided that it merited an official name. Our application to the U.S. Board on Geographic Names required a petition to be signed by at least one hundred people living in the area, along with a support letter from the mayor. We chose the name A. D. Williams Creek, in honor of Martin Luther King Jr.'s maternal grandfather, a minister and civil rights activist for whom the nearby school had been named.

In 2005 our application was approved. Today, all maps identify the stream as A. D. Williams Creek. That spring, we organized a stream-naming ceremony in the middle of the woods beside the creek with local and state officials. The project was tremendously satisfying. Our collective hope to reclaim this pocket of nature in the city kept us working for a better day.

⸜⸝⸜⸝

Not long ago, Neill and I walked through the woods beside A. D. Williams Creek for the first time in a decade. Although we didn't sample the water, it was clear, with none of the distinctive signs or smells of sewage. Trash was minimal. Some tires had been dumped in the upper portion of the stream, not far from the campus of Coretta Scott King Young Women's Leadership Academy, ripe for another cleanup.

Named for the wife of Martin Luther King Jr. and completed in 2007, the academy now sits on the ridge above the creek; my hope is that the school will one day use the forest and creek as an outdoor learning laboratory. The multifamily public housing project, the last large one in Atlanta, was demolished in 2009. The old elementary school was abandoned.

The construction of the King Academy and its athletic field, supported by a massive retaining wall, intrudes somewhat into the old forest. Most of the trees in the creek's steep ravine remain intact: massive white oaks, beeches, hickories, and tulip poplars, along with umbrella magnolias, chestnut oaks, and pines.

Ferns were abundant, as was the sound of birdsong on our walk. On the surface of the stream, we found water striders (Gerridae)—insects also known as water skippers or pond skaters. Darting about on their long, hydrophobic legs, the striders appear to walk on the water as they seek mosquitoes and dragonflies.

I thought again about families and generations: the King family, the families of the convict laborers, my own family, and the beech tree family at Cabin Creek. Too often, we forget that all of us on this planet are one community—that we are all connected by the ties of kinship.

Writer and environmentalist Wallace Stegner argued for the protection of wild lands in his famous 1960 letter to Congress in support of the Wilderness Act. He coined the phrase "a geography of hope" to describe the intrinsic value of these lands, beyond their tangible benefits. I think this notion can be extended to urban lands, particularly places of cultural and natural importance, like the Chattahoochee brickworks site.

Of hope, justice advocate Bryan Stevenson has said: "I am persuaded that hopelessness is the enemy of justice; that if we allow ourselves to become hopeless, we become part of the problem. I think you're either hopeful, or you're the problem. There's no neutral place. . . . Hope is the thing that gets you to stand up, when others say, 'Sit down.' It's the thing that gets you to speak, when others say, 'Be quiet.'"

CHAPTER 28

The Pandemic

Late March to Mid-May, 2020

In February and March, as I continued to explore my path to the river and revel in the early signs of spring, a lethal coronavirus emerged in China and began to spread around the world. By late March, the severity of the virus, named COVID-19, and the uncertainty about how to best manage it, finally became widely known. Shelter-in-place orders were mandated, especially for "elderly" adults (those over sixty-five) like me.

At the beginning of the pandemic, I fell apart for nearly a week. Neill said he'd rarely seen me so stressed and fearful, a fact he reported to my sons. Both of them were about to embark on major trips, which added substantially to my anxiety. Charles and his girlfriend were packed for a cross-country road trip to Oregon, where they would live and work remotely for several months. Robert had plans for a solo surfing trip to Nicaragua on his spring break from teaching.

An article in the *Harvard Business Review* ("That Discomfort You're Feeling Is Grief") helped me walk back from the edge of despair—that and the fact that Robert canceled his surfing trip and Charles promised to be "very careful." David Kessler, a world-renowned expert on grief, explained in the article that what we were experiencing during the early pandemic days was a kind of collective grief: the loss of normalcy, the fear of economic toll, and the loss of connection.

Kessler used a term that resonated with me: "anticipatory grief," the feeling we have about the future when we're uncertain, when our sense of safety is broken. Parents anxious to safeguard their children (or their own parents) from harm could see only the worst scenarios. In my case, sons sick on the West Coast or out of the country with no way for me to get to them.

Kessler wrote that we cannot ignore catastrophic thinking, but we can try to find a sort of balance by coming into the present. By letting go of the things we cannot control. By focusing on what we can manage and realizing that our situation is survivable.

The Chattahoochee River National Recreation Area was closed for two months because of COVID-19. No longer able to walk my trail along Cabin Creek to the river, I imagined what I might have seen as spring unfolded. Memories of past walks helped my mind's eye recall many of the sights, sounds, and smells from these life-affirming rambles. I was also comforted by the certainty and the rhythm of nature. The knowledge that spring will come again to Cabin Creek (and again and again)—and that, eventually, I would be able to return to the ravine and the river. As Rachel Carson observed: "There is something infinitely healing in the repeated refrains of nature—the assurance that dawn comes after night, and spring after winter."

On May 11, 2020, the national park reopened to the public, with admonitions to practice social distancing and wear masks. The people came. Crowds of them. After sheltering in place at home for months, they flocked to the CRNRA and other natural areas throughout the United States and around the world. They hiked, biked, and walked dogs on the trails, connecting with friends and family in the safer outdoors. A similar rush to nature occurred after the 1918 influenza pandemic, with a surge of car-based camping. In fact, so many people visited national parks that it took a toll on the natural landscape. A similar result is being seen in many places today.

A mountain of scientific research has shown that being in nature seems to give the brain permission to relax, while providing the right amount of sensory stimulation. Nature helps decrease anxiety, depression, and fatigue, while improving mood. Studies have also found that natural, anticancer killer cells significantly increase after a long walk in a forest. The therapeutic effects of spending time outside have deepened for many people during this pandemic.

As long as our burdens on her are not too great, nature has an immense capacity to give and to heal.

Mountain laurel (*Kalmia latifolia*), a species of flowering plant in the heath family, blooms along the Chattahoochee River. Photo: Tom Wilson.

CHAPTER 29

Junior, Sparky, and the Poultry Capital of the World

May 14, 2020

When despair for the world grows in me . . .
I go and lie down where the great heron feeds. I come into the peace of wild
things who do not tax their lives with forethought of grief.
I come into the presence of still water. . . .
For a time, I rest in the grace of the world, and am free.
—*Wendell Berry*

In my two-month absence, the woods have become the green forest tunnel that I remember from my first visit a year ago. Paper-thin, elliptical-shaped beech leaves with their distinctive saw-toothed edges have unfurled on their branches. The muted sunlight that easily passes through them casts a pale green light. Direct sunlight no longer reaches the ground, and wildflowers can be found only in patches of sun at the river and near the trailhead, where the tree canopy is less dense.

Blooming foamflowers (*Tiarella cordifolia*) have emerged from the ground near the creeks. Fallen tulip poplar blooms decorate the trail with their greenish-yellow petals and splash of orange at their base. I find a wildflower along the path that is new to me and identify it as yellow star grass (*Hypoxis hirsuta*). The beech family is still there, waiting for me to admire its endurance.

I fail again to find the wildflower Solomon's seal (*Polygonatum*): a shining star of shady woodlands and damp ravines in late spring and summer. I have searched for it on other walks. Bell-like flowers hang in pairs from leaves on the distinctively arching stems of the smooth or true Solomon's seal (*Polygonatum biflorum*). In contrast, false Solomon's seal (*Maianthemum racemosum*), also called feathery false lily of the valley, produces masses of small, pale flowers in flat panicles at the ends of the stems.

My sharp-eyed naturalist friend Kathryn Kolb has found remnants of this perennial plant near Cabin Creek. She believes that deer are feasting on the Solomon's seal: possible evidence of wildlife companions in the ravine, just not companions in time. For most of my short visit, I am alone in the woods and beside the river. The feeling is just as precious as I knew it would be with the green canopy, talking creeks, birdsong, and rich smells. I experience a sense of release like that on the first sunny morning after a long, dark winter.

I look for flowers on the bigleaf magnolias, or evidence of their having bloomed, but all I can see are the massive green leaves that I have come to love. It can take twelve or more years before the large, ivory-colored flowers with rose-purple at the petal base appear on the bigleaf magnolias. By then, the blooms are typically too far from the ground for easy viewing in a forest setting. Perhaps I'll be lucky to find some of the cone-like fruits that mature in late summer and release shiny, red-coated seeds.

It's mountain laurel and rhododendron time again and the laurel bushes are full of pale white blossoms near the river. Back from the trail, closer to the rocky palisades, are the Carolina rhododendron bushes with their exquisite clusters of pink flowers. At the river, which is running high, are several spiderwort plants and another new species for my list. I've found Virginia sweetspire or Virginia willow (*Itea virginica*) leaning dramatically over the water.

By concentrating on the present—on the sensory experiences in my refuge—I am able to put the pandemic turmoil and my fears in some perspective. I attend to the details of trees, rocks, sky, birds, and water. Wild nature endures. It is a constant in the midst of so much other change and sadness.

I reminisce about some of the people who I came to know and respect while working to revive the Chattahoochee. These memorable associations also help alleviate the pandemic uncertainty and despair that now shape our lives.

Junior Arrington of Franklin, Georgia, a small town at the headwaters of West Point Lake, was a singular individual. I met him a year after we started Riverkeeper, when I drove downstream to his rural county for a meeting to talk to local officials about the condition of the Chattahoochee below Atlanta. A huge man, wearing a shirt with sleeves cut off to accommodate his massive arms, suddenly appeared in the doorway of our meeting room. Completely filling its frame, the onetime professional wrestler asked loudly, "Where's the riverkeeper lady?"

Junior said he'd heard about Riverkeeper and its mission to clean up the river. He wanted to help. He remembered when the water in the

Chattahoochee was clean enough to drink. No one knew the river near his hometown better than this big man with a deep laugh, who boasted that he knew every rock and every deep hole in it. Junior had fished the Chattahoochee, hunted its forests, and found Native American artifacts in its floodplains.

He remembered life along the river in the 1940s and 1950s. "We sold catfish to cafes in Hogansville and LaGrange and everywhere else for ten cents a pound. And we trapped muskrats, coons, mink, fox. We trapped 'em, skinned 'em, and stretched 'em on boards until they dried, and along about a month before Christmas, we'd send 'em to Sears Roebuck and they'd send a check back and that's what we'd have Christmas with. Sometimes we'd get four or five hundred dollars. We fished up until the river got so polluted you couldn't do nothing with it."

One of Junior's favorite stories involved protecting the river: "I was sitting up at the shoals fishing, and there was four people drinking beer bottles, and—bam!—throwing 'em against the rocks. I said, 'Hey, don't y'all do that no more. What if a young'un come up here and jumped out and cut off a leg?' One of 'em said, 'Ain't no business of yours!' I ran my big ole bass boat as close as I could get, and I just jumped out and waded over to where they's at. I told 'em, 'I'll turn this boat bottom side up! I better not catch y'all up here doing something like that!'"

When Riverkeeper won the lawsuit against the city of Atlanta in 1997 for its chronic sewage pollution of the river, one of the first people I called was Junior. For me, he represented all the people downstream of the city who deserved a clean river: a place where they could fish and swim and simply enjoy the flow of water on its way to the sea. He was tickled with the victory.

Six years later—while Atlanta was still overhauling its sewer system—Junior died of a heart attack. He was sitting on his front porch swing, looking toward the river he had loved all his life. I wish he were still alive to see how much cleaner the water is today—and that I could thank him again for the work he and so many others started. It has made such a difference.

Ralph Shaw lived 150 miles upstream from Junior in the headwaters region of the Chattahoochee River. He also loved fishing, clean water, and people. His outdoor skills were extraordinary, as was the diversity of his many friends: state officials, wealthy clients who he guided on rivers all over the Southeast, lawyers and activists, academics, and homeless people who he met during a few lost years in the 2000s.

Nicknamed Sparky because he'd been hit twice by lightning, Ralph was a terrific cook. He was steadfastly loyal to the people and places he loved. I learned from him that Georgia's only native trout is the Southern Appalachian brook trout (*Salvelinus fontinalis*) and that it's technically a char: a type of cold-freshwater fish. He thought "brookies" deserved to be a state-protected species, so he formed a group to advocate for their protection. An expert naturalist, he understood the importance of protecting watersheds and high-quality mountain streams.

In the late 1990s, the U.S. Forest Service proposed building a road and clear-cutting an old-growth forest that drains into a brook trout stream near a wilderness area. Its waters flow into the Soque River, then the Chattahoochee. Ralph fought the federal agency in court with his limited resources, telling a reporter, "This creek is so clean and pure. If they go through with this project, it will destroy it. I'm just a redneck trying to do right." He won his case.

I like to think about the generations of brook trout and other species that have lived and thrived in the cold, clean mountain stream because Ralph protected its forested watershed. He was a dedicated environmentalist and a good friend of the Chattahoochee.

Ralph was living in Gainesville, Georgia, "Poultry Capital of the World," in 2009, when I got a call from him one afternoon. He reported a massive fish kill in Flat Creek. The urban stream flows through an industrial area and several neighborhoods, passing schools and churches before entering Lake Lanier. Long considered one of the most polluted waterways in Georgia, Flat Creek was contaminated by various sources, including a sewage plant that failed to meet clean water laws. (It was finally upgraded a few years later.)

We immediately contacted the Georgia Environmental Protection Division to report the fish kill. State employees inspected the creek and evaluated possible sources of the contamination: the pollutants that had depleted oxygen levels in the water and killed the fish and other aquatic species. They ultimately decided there wasn't sufficient evidence to take any action. With several poultry plants located on Flat Creek—slaughtering and processing millions of live chickens every week—we didn't think it was too difficult to imagine what those sources might be. We needed proof.

Intrepid Riverkeeper staff began to monitor the creek, wading into the putrid-smelling water when it rained to collect water samples above and below the plants. We needed to determine whether or not chicken waste was responsible for the high levels of bacteria in the stream. It was not easy or inexpensive to monitor the creek during and after rain events. The uncertainty of weather forecasting and the distance from our Atlanta office to the site made the process complicated.

It took years to collect and process enough data to document the pollution in the storm runoff from the Pilgrim's Pride Corporation and Mar-Jac Poultry facilities. Ultimately, our tests revealed that—when it rained—the bacteria levels in Flat Creek were more than one thousand times the level recommended by the U.S. EPA. At storm drainpipe outfalls on the property of the two poultry plants, the levels were more than ten thousand times the recommended level.

When repeated attempts to work cooperatively with Pilgrim's Pride and Mar-Jac were unsuccessful, Riverkeeper turned to the media and regulatory agencies. Georgia EPD failed to take any meaningful action against the politically powerful companies, so Riverkeeper met with the U.S. EPA and provided the collected data. Subsequently, EPA conducted unannounced investigations of the chicken facilities and issued a damning report in 2015.

The report stated, "Feathers, blood and maggots litter the pavement and clog pipes that are supposed to convey only rainwater from the site to Flat Creek. Trucks carrying thousands of caged chickens are sprayed with water, which mingles with chicken feces and runs off to a pipe draining directly into the creek." At the beginning of the federal inspection, Pilgrim's Pride representatives had told EPA agents that all of their drainpipes went to the Gainesville wastewater treatment system or into city storm drains. They didn't. Several led directly to the creek.

⌒⌒⌒

In 2016, seven years after Ralph reported the fish kill, EPA settled with Pilgrim's Pride. The agency required the company to spend more than $1 million to capture the dirtiest stormwater flowing from its site in a massive storage tank. The wastewater would then be pretreated and sent to the city's sewage plant for additional treatment before being discharged into the creek.

No longer would the company's chicken waste, blood, and feathers flow directly into a public waterway and a lake that annually draws millions of people for recreation. A new environmental manager arrived at Pilgrim's Pride a year later, and the company began to work cooperatively with Riverkeeper and EPA to remediate its problems. Mar-Jac was also fined and required to take action to improve its stormwater control practices. Riverkeeper staff and volunteers continue to monitor Flat Creek, where they have found and reported other sources of contamination in the industrial area. Slowly but surely the creek is being revived.

In the intervening years, Ralph, who had been in poor health, died, never knowing that his vigilance and commitment to protecting the natural environment had resulted in such a major accomplishment. The powerful poultry industry had been forced to abide by clean water laws, just like everyone else.

CHAPTER 30

No Longer Voiceless

May 22, 2020

Though I die, though I lose my life, nature wins. Nature endures. It is strange and it is hard, but it is comfort and I'll take it.
—*Eva Saulitis*

My intention on my walk today is to take additional measurements to learn more about the beech tree family that has been sustained by the forest and streams in the Cabin Creek watershed. The woods are humid, but the air by the river is cool and breezy, causing small whitecaps on the water, which is bank full from recent heavy rain.

A few wildflowers remain where the sun still reaches the canopy-shaded ground. Mountain laurel flowers near the river are beginning to wilt in the warmer temperatures. Blooms on laurels and rhododendrons on the steep slope above the trail still look fresh.

Birds are singing as I wrap my tape measure around the girth of the large "father" beech tree, which grows several yards from the fallen mother beech and her offspring. With a circumference of eighty-four inches, the tree is roughly 160 years old. It could have begun growing around 1860, as the American Civil War began. I wonder if this healthy beech, or any of the other nearby trees, have provided water, nutrients, and sugars to support the fallen tree and her offspring, through the vast underground fungal networks. Again, I ponder how long it will be before the mother tree turns into nutrient-rich humus and largely disappears. Forest time is slow. Much patience is required of human observers.

Near the creek, I take another look at the beech tree with the large hollow that I found on an earlier walk. It's the second-largest beech that I've discovered in the forest. I estimate it to be about 180 years old. The small beech growing from one of its surface roots may be nearly three decades old. As beeches age, the interior wood often rots, leaving hollow areas that provide excellent den sites for squirrels, raccoons, and opossums.

Hundreds of ants are climbing up and down the beech tree trunk. Are they looking for a cavity in which to nest, or searching for woolly beech aphids (*Phyllaphis fagi*)? Ants "farm" aphids in some trees, protecting them and their trees from other insects, in order to enjoy honeydew: a sweet, sticky substance produced by the aphids.

Nature never fails to surprise me. There is so much to celebrate in the diversity and persistence of life. Whatever ultimately happens to *Homo sapiens* in the centuries and millennia to come, nature will endure, and that is indeed a comfort.

I hiked alone at dusk into the Mark Trail Wilderness, seeking the spring that gives birth to the Chattahoochee, where, the next morning, my friends Joe Cook and Monica Sheppard would start their one-hundred-day journey down the river to the Gulf of Mexico.

Guided by a note they left at the trailhead, I knew that the couple was already at Chattahoochee Gap, where we would camp. I had several more miles to go before I would reach them. Trying to keep my mind off the descending darkness, I focused on the valley below with its pinpoints of bright light and contemplated the previous year, 1994, my first as the Chattahoochee's riverkeeper. So many challenges, but great satisfaction as well.

I had finally found my passion and a life-changing career. As the mother of two sons, I had already found the most important, consequential, and fulfilling experience of my life. My riverkeeping job gave me the chance to make another sort of difference, as an advocate for a river that sustains millions of people, including my family, and wildlife.

At Chattahoochee Gap, after a little food and excited conversation about the couple's adventures to come, I lay my sleeping bag on the ground next to the Appalachian Trail. The two-thousand-plus-mile path passes directly through the gap on its way from Georgia to Maine. Lying several hundred feet upslope of the river's birthplace—the tiny spring of pristine water surrounded by mosses and ferns—I fell asleep in the chilly mountain air.

The next morning, I wished the couple well on their journey and hiked back to my car.

Twenty years passed in what seemed like a flash. I was standing on a stage in a fancy hotel ballroom in Atlanta that contained six hundred friends, family, and supporters, celebrating Riverkeeper's twentieth anniversary and my retirement.

As the gala began, my stomach was in knots. I literally felt like I was going to be sick. It was so important to do a good job of thanking everyone who had helped Riverkeeper over the years and introducing Jason Ulseth, the new riverkeeper, and Juliet Cohen, the new executive director. Both were trusted veteran staff with fire in their bellies who would take over the leadership reins. I wanted to make sure that everyone knew these extraordinary individuals had my full confidence, respect, and support to launch Riverkeeper into its third decade. My sister offered me something to calm my upset stomach. I gave my speech.

After I finished speaking, Alice Champagne and Denise Donahue came on stage with me. A mother of two small children who wanted to help save the Chattahoochee (and did), Alice was my first hire at Riverkeeper. Denise, a longtime Riverkeeper board member, taught me how to put my hopes and plans for the river into words and images with her graphic design skills and endless generosity.

They were joined by the Riverkeeper staff to announce that the little stream behind my childhood home would henceforth be named Riverkeeper Creek on all official maps. With a lump in my throat and tears pricking my eyes, I thanked them with words now forgotten, but feelings of gratitude that will remain the rest of my life.

While I would no longer be at the helm of the effort to protect our life-giving river, I knew that the journey we embarked on so long ago would stay on course and succeed. The Chattahoochee River and the streams that sustain it are no longer voiceless.

CHAPTER 31

Mushrooms and State Legislators

September 2, 2020

After I completed my year of walks through the forested ravine along Cabin Creek to the Chattahoochee in May of 2020, I found myself continuing to wonder what was happening in that pocket of nature I had come to know so well. Were the tiny fish still darting about in the elbow of the creek, not far from newly built crayfish chimneys? Was the lavender-colored downy lobelia near the mouth of Cabin Creek in bloom yet? Had the otter made another appearance, cavorting and fishing in the river's shoals?

To satisfy my curiosity and keep myself grounded in the present, as the COVID-19 pandemic continued its tragic trajectory, I kept returning to the woods and the river. Acting upon author Robin Wall Kimmerer's advice, I catalogued the seasonal changes in my journal. "Writing is an act of reciprocity with the living land. Words to remember old stories, words to tell new ones, stories that bring science and spirit back together," Kimmerer wrote in *Braiding Sweetgrass*.

Weatherwise, the summer and fall of 2020 were quite different from the year before. Heavy rains dominated the summer months and early fall, resulting in a massive bloom of mushrooms: the colorful fruiting bodies of fungi.

I walk through the woods to the river with my eyes wide open, alert for the mushrooms that I assume will be poking out of the forest floor after months of rain. I am not disappointed: they are everywhere, displaying vivid colors and fascinating shapes. I find mushrooms with thick, light brown, flat caps that look like small—and some not so small—pancakes. Others have red caps with white dots and pale yellow stalks (*Amanita muscaria*, commonly known as fly agaric) that resemble mushrooms from the Nintendo game Super Mario.

Another mushroom variety is bright yellow; a dozen individuals are growing in a semicircle under laurel bushes near the river. Could this be a fairy ring of sorts? Several bulbous red-capped fungi (without dots) have not yet fully emerged from their white volvas or egg sacs (*Amanita jacksonii*). Every time I find one of these *Amanita*, I feel like I've found a treasure; even more so when they are in a cluster.

Dozens of pure white mushrooms congregate near the creek, some with chunks missing from their caps. Perhaps a hungry critter has chewed off the pieces. Tiny white fungi on long stalks pierce an oak leaf lying on the ground. Hundreds of fruiting bodies are decorating the woods. There is so much life underground that can make itself partially visible to human eyes, when the conditions are just right.

While the fungi are my primary focus on today's walk, I'm excited to find my first seed pod from a bigleaf magnolia lying on the ground. It's the size of a fist with fleshy red seeds; they would have popped out of the pod in several months if it had been allowed to ripen on the tree. Perhaps it was knocked out of the magnolia by a storm or a rambunctious animal.

At the Chattahoochee, dark purple butterflies drink nectar from blooming joe-pye weed stalks. Sweet autumn clematis (*Clematis terniflora*), a nonnative perennial vine from Asia, exhibits its spidery white flowers in the sun along the riverbank. The river is full and noisy today as it rushes over and around the rocks and islands that stand in its way.

As a child, I loved Kenneth Grahame's *The Wind in the Willows*. After recently finding an old copy in a used bookstore, I read it again—enjoying, as much as ever, the river adventures of Ratty, Mole, Badger, and Mr. Toad. On my walks at the Chattahoochee, I often think of one passage: "[Mole] sat on the bank, while the river chattered on to him, a babbling procession of the best stories in the world, sent from the heart of the earth to be told at last to the insatiable sea."

Not unlike the many varieties of mushrooms I find today—which have emerged suddenly from the ground after this year's rainy season—our elected state representatives, 236 in total, appear like magic at the state capitol in Atlanta every January. They travel there from all parts of Georgia.

The state capitol in downtown Atlanta, with its shiny dome gilded with native gold leaf mined in north Georgia, was never my favorite place to work on behalf of Georgia's rivers. Despite my lack of enthusiasm, when the legislature convened, I would put on my business suit, pearls, and heels and join the circus.

For many years, whenever I entered the capitol, I was immediately confused, uncertain which direction to walk to find my destination. Far too often, I walked in circles, pretending I knew where I was going, until I learned to look for the larger-than-life bust of James Oglethorpe. Once I saw the founder of the colony of Georgia, I could navigate the rest of the way.

With its marble floors and limited seating, the capitol is a physically uncomfortable place to spend time. Worse, the byzantine process by which bills are introduced, evaluated, and passed is more than a little challenging and frustrating. I never understood it all, relying instead on Juliet, then Riverkeeper's general counsel, and veteran lobbyists Neill Herring and Mark Woodall. They thrive on the whirlwind of activity, even during the last three days of the forty-day legislative session, when the backroom dealing reaches a fever pitch.

Lobbyists hang out on the third floor of the building, watching televisions that show the activity in each legislative chamber (House and Senate). This makes them easily accessible to legislators, who periodically dash out of their chamber doors to ask for advice or meet with constituents.

Public interest lobbyists who advocate for the environment, healthcare, families, education, and other progressive causes can be found on the north side of the third floor (above Oglethorpe). Business lobbyists dominate the south side of the building with its shoe-shine stand—a deep, philosophical (and compensation) chasm between them.

On the last day of the session, which typically ends at midnight, the legislators throw their papers into the air simultaneously and run, literally, out of the chambers. It was always my favorite part of every session. A whole year would have to pass before we would need to again mount campaigns to fight environmentally damaging bills and try to pass a few protective ones.

During the 1990s and early 2000s, Riverkeeper and colleagues collaborated frequently with a number of influential Republican leaders in the state legislature, including former senator Mike Egan from Atlanta and former senator Chuck Clay from Marietta. They understood that a healthy economy and environment are not mutually exclusive. Clean air, land, and water are bipartisan issues—or they should be.

Since 2005, when both the Georgia House and Senate became Republican majorities for the first time since Reconstruction, the Republican leadership has largely been controlled by pro-growth, anti-environmental interests. Our work has become increasingly difficult and more frustrating.

The Georgia Water Coalition works tirelessly to defeat bills harmful to our waterways and land, often with a variety of allies. During my riverkeeping years, the coalition stopped legislative proposals that would have allowed greater secrecy for polluters, reduced the public's right to know about the health of their communities, and chilled whistleblower reporting.

When the ability of citizens to challenge environmental permits came under attack, we stopped that misguided effort. We safeguarded waterways by defeating bills that would have supported the damming of a major tributary to the Chattahoochee, weakened stream buffer protections, and reduced requirements to control soil erosion.

The Georgia Department of Transportation, the biggest dirt-mover in the state, repeatedly asked the legislature to exempt the agency and its contractors from erosion control laws and fines for violations. We defeated each of these attempts. Our most significant legislative battle was over water permit trading or water marketing—a huge win for the coalition and all state waters (described in chapter 24).

The coalition's successful, proactive initiatives before my retirement ranged from reforming Georgia's erosion control program and adopting citizen water sampling protocols to enacting greater riverbank protection along a thirty-four-mile section of the Chattahoochee and the first state water management plan. Other victories mandated water efficiency measures to reduce overuse and stress on waterways, improved statewide buffer laws, helped fund Atlanta's overhaul of its sewer system through a municipal option sales tax, and mandated funds for emergency response to environmental disasters.

My decades at the state capitol taught me many things, but the most important lesson was to ditch high heels for comfortable shoes, no matter what they look like. More relevant to the work: the chairs of House legislative committees (appointed by the Speaker of the House) can make or break the success of advocacy. For example, Representative Lynn Smith—a longtime chair of the natural resources committee and a Republican from Newnan—is infamous for refusing to hold any hearings on bills not supported by her party's leaders. Regularly, she strangles environmental legislation before it can even be discussed, much less voted on, while often indulging state-regulated businesses and utilities.

Other lessons learned: If a bill isn't going to pass, meaning the primary bill sponsors are minority party representatives, don't spend time and energy trying to perfect the bill. And, importantly, it is essential to overlook positions on other issues that may be held by legislators who support your environmental projects, even if you personally oppose their nonenvironmental views. Stay focused on your goals.

Finally, encouraging a legislator's constituents to contact their legislator in support of your bill is critical. While lobbyists for nonprofits are often asked for advice and assistance, it is the local folks who can really make the difference in a bill's success or failure. This is particularly true if those local folks are members of the Garden Club of Georgia, who know the legislator's mama. Personal relationships can be as important as a well-crafted argument in favor of your position—more so, in many instances.

CHAPTER 32

Indescribable Joy

October 16, 2020

For the first time since I retired from Riverkeeper in 2014, I walk down the Georgia Highway 166 boat ramp, slippery with mud from recent heavy rains, and climb onto the Riverkeeper patrol boat. On a similar morning more than twenty-five years ago, I met Gandy Glover downstream at the Coweta County boat ramp for my first extensive tour of the Chattahoochee below Atlanta. It was an experience I'll never forget. It was when I began to fall in love with the long-blighted river between the city and West Point Lake: its forested banks, rocky shoals, islands, and wildlife.

There was a time—when this section of the river was still heavily polluted—that the Georgia Department of Natural Resources opposed the building of any boat ramps. Its policy was to discourage public recreation in the contaminated waters. The agency apparently assumed the river would never be cleaned up.

As sewer overflows upstream in Atlanta abated with the mandated overhaul of the city's sewer system, the state built this ramp at Highway 166. Years passed and the river became dramatically cleaner with the completion of more major sewer improvements. A second state boat ramp opened at Campbellton Park in the city of Chattahoochee Hills in 2020.

Our resilient river has returned.

The morning weather is chilly and overcast as we begin the eighteen-mile journey upriver to Peachtree Creek with Jason at the jet boat's helm. The muddy residue imprinted on shrubs, trees, and land many feet above the current water level reveals how high the river has been in recent days, well over her banks and across her floodplain. Although the Chattahoochee is lower now, she is still much higher than normal. Pieces of wood bob up and down in the fast-moving water, mixed with leaves and some trash.

Occasionally, we stop to remove debris that is clogging the jet motor. These interludes allow me time to more closely observe the sycamore trees that majestically line the banks, just as I remembered them. Their leaves are turning brown and yellow in the cooler weather: drifting from branches into the water, exposing more of the stark, white bark—white as bone or ivory—in the upper portion of these beauties.

Late afternoon reflections in the Chattahoochee River among the author's "frozen waves."
Photo: Tom Wilson.

Near the confluence of Nickajack Creek and the river, we slow down and stop to hear Jason's story about a Civil War historian. Using a magnetic device, he pulled horseshoes, chains, and horse-drawn buggy parts from the Chattahoochee's bottom into the Riverkeeper boat. For more than 150 years, these relics had lain in the sand and mud, as boats passed above them—initially powered by poles, paddles, and oars, then a variety of combustion engines, later waterjet propulsion. Each with increasing efficiency and power.

Nickajack marks the southernmost reaches of Johnston's River Line, built to stop the Union Army's siege of Atlanta during the war. On July 9, 1864, the Union successfully crossed the Chattahoochee far upstream, forcing a Confederate retreat to the south side of the river.

According to *Chattahoochee River User's Guide*, the two armies rested and put down their arms here for several days: "Facing one another across the cool, inviting waters, and dirty from weeks of fighting, soldiers from both sides stripped and plunged into the river to bathe and swim; newspapers were exchanged and southern tobacco was traded for northern coffee. A week later, they would return to killing each other."

We continue our journey upstream, passing Buzzard Roost Island—where archaeological evidence confirms that humans have crossed the river for at least twelve thousand years—and stop to admire what Jason calls a "Sally sign." Above an outfall pipe, the sign provides information about the discharge of treated sewage here; an emergency phone number is provided, should any boater or fisher need to report a problem. The signage is required by the policy approved when I was a member of the Georgia Board of Natural Resources.

Approaching a half-mile stretch along the Chattahoochee, once crowded with small commercial and industrial facilities, I am amazed to find the first phase of a new, upscale apartment complex. Eventually, coworking space, retail stores, and single-family homes will become part of this community. Its promoters describe the development as a "walkable waterfront oasis." A twelve-acre park along the river includes a kayak launch and public dock.

No longer is this riverbank overflowing with waste and rubble from industrial activities, its condition as recently as a decade ago. No longer is the Chattahoochee so polluted here that no real estate developer in their right mind would make an investment. The river corridor downstream of Atlanta is becoming a place where people want to live and recreate.

The clouds have moved on and we are bathed in bright sun with blue skies above as we continue motoring upstream past the Georgia Power plant, once coal fired and now generating electricity with natural gas. Millions of tons of coal ash remain on site, buried in groundwater next to the river.

Containing dangerous heavy metals and carcinogens, coal ash is the byproduct of burning coal. Riverkeeper has long advocated that this toxic material be excavated and disposed of properly—away from groundwater and surface waters. In 2022 the U.S. EPA announced a plan to require more stringent rules regarding ash disposal, including its removal from groundwater. Georgia Power and other utilities are seeking to block this EPA action. Riverkeeper and its partners have intervened in the legal case.

I see the old, closed landfill, where we once collected a water sample before our boat-sinking adventure. The city's upgraded Clayton sewage treatment plant—where condoms once decorated the nearby trees—comes into view. We pass the asphalt plant, where we worked with the owner to reduce industrial pollutants in storm runoff. Then we travel over the spot where a huge sewage spill boiled up in the middle of the river, forcing a reporter and me to jump back into the boat to escape the filth.

We cruise under a Western & Atlanta Railroad bridge built in the 1840s; during the Civil War, it was the only bridge across the river near Atlanta. Ahead is a major intersection in the Chattahoochee: the place where Peachtree Creek, which drains much of downtown Atlanta, enters the river. Immediately upstream, the city withdraws more than one hundred million gallons of water daily to sustain people and businesses. Across the river and slightly downstream, a Cobb County plant with a Sally sign empties treated sewage into the river.

An eagle flies over the Chattahoochee and lands at the top of a tall sycamore tree on De-Foors Island, where long ago we sought refuge after the boat-sinking episode. As we slowly motor into the flooded mouth of Peachtree Creek, a great blue heron with a wingspan of at least five feet flies just above our heads. In the soft breeze, leaves fall from the overhanging trees into the nearly motionless stream.

In the high river water, it's easy for our boat to pass over the rock weir built by the city to pool water for withdrawal at its intake. We enter the lower portion of the Chattahoochee River National Recreation Area and pause for a few minutes, watching the bank-full river split at the island. Then we turn around and head back downstream.

Standing behind the helm and holding on to a metal rail as we speed down river—with the wind whipping my hair, the sun warm on my face, and river smells recharging my brain—I feel an indescribable joy. The feel and smell of memory. If only we could keep going, all the way to Apalachicola.

At a riverside park, we meet Juliet and the rest of the Riverkeeper staff for a picnic lunch: a pandemic-safe way to reconnect and catch up with each other after long days and months of working from home. As we laugh and talk by the river's side, she flows steadily on—linking the mountains with the sea, carrying memories of all that has gone before, and waiting patiently for what is yet to come.

AFTERWORD

Chattahoochee Riverkeeper's mission has been simple and straightforward from the beginning: to advocate and secure the protection and stewardship of the Chattahoochee River and its watershed. Specifically, the organization works to restore and conserve the river system's ecological health for the people and wildlife that depend on her for their survival.

The Chattahoochee connects us to our past and to our future, to our neighbors upstream and down, and to the natural world of fish and wildlife. Thousands of donors—large and small—invested nearly $30 million in Chattahoochee Riverkeeper during its first twenty-five years to support this critical work, understanding the value of nature's many services. That investment and a great deal of hard work led to a transformation of the river that provides drinking water for more than five million people—and so much more.

In celebration of the organization's twenty-fifth anniversary in 2019, Riverkeeper staff compiled a record of our most significant accomplishments. We found that our actions had resulted in more than $2.2 billion in benefits to the Chattahoochee watershed, people, and wildlife. Today, our river is viewed in a whole new light—as an amenity rather than a drainage ditch for the waste from one of the largest metropolitan regions in the Southeast. Chattahoochee Riverkeeper's successes are leading to cleaner water, better health for people and wildlife, and more equitable communities.

On countless other water bodies around the world, increasing numbers of people are fighting effectively in courtrooms, town hall meetings, legislatures, and classrooms—and in the streets, when necessary. They are demanding that their community waterways be protected from ignorance, apathy, and greed. Having enough clean water is a basic human right.

ACKNOWLEDGMENTS

I was privileged to grow up with parents who loved the natural world and did what they could to protect wild places like Sanibel Island. My parents, Helen and Joe Sierer, both instilled an appreciation for nature in me. In his actions, my father showed me the importance of being an advocate. Through books and her art, my mother reinforced nature's beauty and resilience.

Laura Turner Seydel and Rutherford Seydel took a chance and gave me the opportunity of a lifetime to become Riverkeeper's founding director nearly thirty years ago—as did both of their caring and generous families. I always knew they had my back, personally and professionally. For that I will be forever grateful. Their leadership, guidance, and resources over more than a quarter of a century continue to be instrumental to Riverkeeper's ongoing success.

For two decades, Riverkeeper's exceptional board of directors—all volunteers—served as mentors, strategists, and cheerleaders for me and the staff. Together, we worked hard, played hard, made difficult decisions, celebrated victories, and kept the organization's mission to safeguard the Chattahoochee River at the forefront at all times. They made me a better manager and communicator, a stronger fundraiser, and a tougher negotiator. This book is their story as much as mine and the dedicated Riverkeeper staff's.

The intelligent, passionate, and hardworking individuals who staffed Riverkeeper during my years with the organization formed the foundation of our success. Much gratitude to Alex Adams, Katherine Baer, Tammy Bates, Birgit Bolton, Alice Champagne, Magnus Christon, Juliet Cohen, Kristin Costley, Bill Crawford, Pam Davee, Michelle Craig DeVoe, Erin Gallagher Dufy, Page Gleason, Mary O. Harrison, Laura Hartt, Kristi Rose Hastie, Skelly Holmbeck, Duncan Hughes, Bonnie Jackson, Henry Jacobs, Matt Kales, Rebecca Klein, Sandy Layton, Mary Manson, Michele Merkel, Mike Meyer, David Moore, Betsy Nicholas, Clare Richie, David Lee Simmons, Jill Sistino, Dana Poole Skelton,

Susan Smith, Jess Sterling, D.J. Strickland, Harlan Trammell, Jason Ulseth, Mary Johnson Woosley, and Christina York. Hundreds of Riverkeeper interns also supported our work over the years. Proudly, many of them successfully pursued environmental careers with government agencies, law firms, consulting companies, and local and national nonprofit organizations.

Effective river advocacy depends on securing accurate, timely information. It can be difficult, however, for the public and nonprofit organizations to access the necessary data and other relevant material from government agencies. I am extremely grateful to the hundreds of people with local, state, and federal agencies who continue to answer questions from Riverkeeper staff, find documents, and interpret scientific studies. They include exceptional biologists, hydrologists, engineers, ecologists, environmental educators, fishery and wildlife managers, foresters, urban planners, geologists, environmental lawyers, and climatologists.

The Forest Unseen: A Year's Watch in Nature by David George Haskell motivated my year of walking the Cabin Creek trail through the national park to the Chattahoochee River. Following Haskell, I wanted to observe nature through the seasons, paying attention to the small things we often miss. As I walked, I remembered: stories from two decades of working to revive our great southern river. I decided that these were tales I wanted to tell.

As for the nuts and bolts of producing this book, I found early and much-needed encouragement from Susan Percy, Teresa Weaver, Janisse Ray, and Dorinda Dallmeyer. They gave me the confidence to keep writing and rewriting, urging me to dig deeper and tell more personal stories. Helping ensure readability and accuracy, while jogging my memory, were knowledgeable book reviewers: Kathryn Kolb, Chris Manganiello, Bill Witherspoon, Diane Badger, Julie Owens, Holly Korschun, Juliet Cohen, Jason Ulseth, and Charles Bethea. Collin Kelley, editor of *Atlanta Intown*, gave me the opportunity to write monthly environmental columns beginning in 2015. I honed my writing and communication skills over the years with his support and guidance.

Wonderful nature photographers—Tom Wilson, Henry Jacobs, Alan Cressler, Lucie Langford Canfield, Don Hunter, Justin Dobson, and Bard

Wrisley—generously provided the images that illustrate this book. Monica Sheppard assisted with design aspects of the book. Editors Patrick Allen and Nate Holly, copyeditor Sarah C. Smith, and the team at the University of Georgia Press guided me through every step of the book publishing process with excellent advice, patience, and good humor.

My partner, Neill Herring, was an integral part of the development of this book. He read every word, several times, provided masterful edits, and joined me on my walks. His extensive knowledge of many topics, and talent for finding the exact word when I needed it, have made this book richer and more interesting.

Finally, I would be remiss not to mention that one of the (very few) positive things that materialized for me during the COVID-19 pandemic was this book. As I spent extended periods alone in my house, sheltering in place, the pandemic provided time—plenty of time—for me to read wonderful, inspiring nature books and write this memoir. It was a joy to remember and write, as the hours often passed like minutes.

A CHRONOLOGY: CHATTAHOOCHEE RIVERKEEPER HIGHLIGHTS (1994–2016)

1994 Laura Turner Seydel and Rutherford Seydel cofound Upper Chattahoochee Riverkeeper (later renamed Chattahoochee Riverkeeper, CRK) and hire Sally Bethea as riverkeeper and executive director. Turner Foundation provides start-up grant. CRK opens office in Atlanta, selects first board of directors, develops strategic action plan, and creates Citizen Response Hotline.

1995 CRK and downstream plaintiffs file lawsuit in federal court against the city of Atlanta for chronic sewage spills into the Chattahoochee River. CRK initiates cleanup of leaking underground storage tanks to stop gasoline from seeping into the river near Helen and acquires first motorized patrol boat. Secretary of the Interior Bruce Babbitt visits Chattahoochee River National Recreation Area to promote urban parks. Joe Cook and Monica Sheppard paddle down the length of the river in one hundred days.

1996 CRK Headwaters office opens in Gainesville, Georgia. Industrial stormwater pollution at Matthews asphalt facility is resolved, setting precedent for hundreds of similar cleanups at industrial sites throughout Chattahoochee Basin. State withdraws memo attempting, illegally, to exempt intermittent streams from buffer protection. CRK initiates watershed town hall meeting series and creates first website.

1997 Federal Judge Thomas Thrash concludes it to be a "matter of undisputed fact" that Atlanta has violated the federal Clean Water Act in discharges from its sewage facilities. Lawsuit against town of Cornelia is settled, resolving chronic pollution of tributary from high levels of nitrogen and ammonia (chicken waste) and requiring major upgrades to sewage plant.

The Riverkeeper's Guide to the Chattahoochee is published. CRK helps secure provisions to protect water quality and ecology in the Apalachicola-Chattahoochee-Flint Basin during water conflict negotiations.

1998   State Metro River Protection Act is extended thirty-four miles downstream of Atlanta and national park, regulating development in the river corridor. U.S. EPA joins CRK's litigation against Atlanta to help compel the city to overhaul its entire sewer system; case is settled with consent decree requiring compliance with federal law by dates certain, amended in 1999. State takes action against town of Clarkesville after reports of chronic problems at sewage facilities from overflows of sewage and medical waste into Soque River. Five-year drought begins in metro Atlanta.

1999   Atlanta completes massive trash cleanup in thirty-seven miles of city streams, per the federal consent decree, with 568 tons of debris removed. CRK completes Soque River Restoration Project; produces video and outreach materials. Enforcement actions are taken to stop chronic releases of high levels of nitrogen and ammonia (chicken waste) from municipal sewage plant into a tributary. Palmetto is forced to upgrade failing sewage facilities and manage excessive flows from mobile home parks. Bethea is appointed to Georgia Board of Natural Resources by newly elected governor Roy Barnes. Bethea and others tasked by Barnes with negotiating a compromise solution to regulate and protect buffers along trout streams in north Georgia.

2000   CRK establishes floating classroom program on Lake Lanier, partnering with Elachee Nature Science Center. Creates BacteriALERT Monitoring Program in partnership with USGS and National Park Service to monitor water quality in CRNRA. Ongoing sewage spill into the river from large pipe is discovered in remote section of Cobb County. Conservation groups convene Georgia Citizen's Water Summit and adopt Water Bill of Rights, setting the stage for creation of Georgia Water Coalition.

2001   Connally Nature Park is preserved and a restoration plan is initiated. CRK and the state create fish consumption outreach campaign to increase awareness of problems with eating contaminated fish. New state policy requires municipal and industrial dischargers to install signs at discharge outfalls. Standing (legal right) is established in Georgia Power Plant Wansley case, allowing third parties to appeal state water withdrawal permits: a precedent. Department of Audits issues damning report about Georgia's erosion control program. Metro North Georgia Water Planning District is created, using Clean Water Initiative recommendations with CRK input.

2002   CRK and three other nonprofits establish the Georgia Water Coalition. Judge in the appeal of Plant Wansley's water withdrawal permit finds in CRK favor—that Georgia Power did not need all the river water it requested—then reverses with little explanation. Shirley Franklin begins the first of her two terms as mayor of Atlanta.

2003   The Georgia Water Coalition achieves significant victory at the state capitol: waterways will continue to be protected as a public resource, not a marketable commodity. Legislature passes historic amendments to state erosion control laws to reform and fund this environmental program. CRK inaugurates Back to the Chattahoochee River Race and Festival. Aquatic biodiversity study discovers rare fishes in Chattahoochee headwaters.

2004   Georgia Supreme Court issues landmark interpretation of Clean Water Act, leading to stronger pollution control technologies to protect Lake Lanier's high-quality waters. CRK coproduces award-winning Waters to the Sea educational tool. National Park Service proposes flawed management plan for CRNRA; CRK and sportsmen's groups help secure a much-improved plan. CRK celebrates tenth anniversary with gala honoring Ted Turner and others.

2005   CRK initiates Get the Dirt Out program. A. D. Williams Creek is officially named. Georgia Department of Corrections is held accountable for pollution from construction at new detention facility. Georgia Power is found to be in violation of state buffer law and is required to secure state approval for future waterfront construction. CRK completes study of metro Atlanta trends in hard surface development and tree canopy loss.

2006   Exceptional drought begins in metro Atlanta, resulting in nineteen-foot drop in level of Lake Lanier; this drought lasts until early 2009. Nancy Creek tunnel is completed, stopping sewer overflows in major tributary. State admits Lake Lanier is "impaired" based on CRK data analysis and is forced to develop a cleanup plan. Camo Coalition creates Angler's Pocket Guide to Erosion and Sediment Control using Get the Dirt Out program materials.

2007   CRK purchases custom-built catamaran for floating classroom on Lake Lanier. Files legal action to stop contamination at riverfront landfill in north Atlanta and secures remediation. Protects stream buffers at multiple sites from development with enforcement actions and defends buffer laws at state capitol. State senators remove Bethea from the Board of Natural Resources after seven years of service, based on a false claim that she cannot be a registered lobbyist and also serve on the board.

2008   Atlanta's Greenway Acquisition Program is completed per CRK's federal consent decree, protecting nearly two thousand acres of riparian land from development. CRK develops No Time to Waste program to promote water conservation with "Tapped Out" presentation, "Filling the Water Gap" report, Rain Barrel program, and more. Manages removal of four tons of trash, made visible by the exceptional drought, from Lake Lanier. Creates River Discovery Series for paddlers in CRNRA.

2009   Major fish kill in tributary to Lake Lanier sparks a multiyear effort to stop pollution at poultry processing facilities. CRK initiates nutrient monitoring program at ten locations on Lake Lanier. U.S. District Court judge issues "draconian" order related to metro Atlanta water supply. ACF Stakeholders Group is established with CRK as a board member. Upper

Chattahoochee Water Trail report is completed. Epic flood submerges Atlanta's Clayton sewage treatment plant, built nearly one hundred years earlier in a floodplain.

2010 CRK creates Neighborhood Water Watch Program to train volunteers to collect water samples weekly in urban streams for bacteria analysis; installs state-of-the-art labs later in all three CRK offices. Lawsuit is settled for clean water violations at Cumming aquatic center, requiring the restoration of a tributary to Lake Lanier, environmental education programs, and the funding of water quality projects. CRK appeals state permit allowing Forsyth County to discharge treated sewage from its Fowler/Shakerag sewage plant into CRNRA.

2011 CRK opens Middle Chattahoochee office in LaGrange, Georgia. Publishes first "Filling the Water Gap" report. Creates annual Sweep the Hooch Cleanup with government and nonprofit partners. Is named the number-one Adopt-a-Stream group in Georgia for most water samples collected—still at the top in 2022. Submits substantial comments regarding Hall County application to dam a Chattahoochee tributary for private real estate development.

2012 The Chattahoochee is named third-most-endangered river in the country for threats posed by proposed dams and reservoirs. CRK receives highly competitive grant from U.S. EPA to expand Neighborhood Water Watch Program. Atlanta is allowed to extend final sewer consent decree deadline to 2027 due to recession, droughts, and high burden on taxpayers. Major leak in Atlanta's drinking water system is found and fixed. The river within the national park is designated first national water trail.

2013 CRK creates new program to tackle industrial stormwater pollution at hundreds of sites throughout the river basin: Protecting Streams and Communities from Industrial Pollution. Floating classroom program is recognized with naming of CRK and Elachee Nature Science Center as Georgia Project WET Organizations of the Year. Georgia Supreme Court rejects CRK petition for review, denying the organization's appeal of Forsyth sewage plant permit; four-year effort to protect national park waters ends largely in disappointment. Georgia DOT is forced to comply with federal stormwater requirements in all road construction statewide.

2014   All major capital improvement projects are completed to upgrade Atlanta's sewer system pursuant to the federal consent decree, with extensions granted for some projects. CRK initiates capacity-building campaign to raise $2 million to expand programs in its third decade. Holds twentieth-anniversary gala to honor Sally Bethea, who retired at end of the year. Jason Ulseth and Juliet Cohen are promoted to riverkeeper and executive director, respectively.

2015   CRK establishes second floating classroom on West Point Lake for schools and community groups in the Middle Chattahoochee region. ACF Stakeholders Group issues sustainable water management plan after six years of intense negotiations. One of the highest environmental penalties in Georgia history ($10 million) is imposed upon American Sealcoat for releasing toxic waste into the river; the property owner is forced to conduct site cleanup and restoration when Sealcoat employees flee the state.

2016   Federal enforcement actions are taken against two major poultry processing companies in Gainesville, seven years after first investigated. The Glades dam and reservoir proposed for a tributary in the Upper Chattahoochee is put on hold by the state; Hall County withdraws permit request. CRK collects 4,256 Neighborhood Water Watch samples, manages 258 hotline calls with 20 related enforcement actions, conducts 110 field investigations, and stops 16 sewage spills.

RESOURCES

Local and Regional Organizations

Apalachicola Riverkeeper (www.apalachicolariverkeeper.org) is dedicated to the protection, restoration, and stewardship of the Apalachicola River and Bay in Florida.

Chattahoochee National Park Conservancy (www.chattahoocheeparks .org) is the official friends group for the Chattahoochee River National Recreation Area.

Chattahoochee Nature Center (www.chattnaturecenter.org) connects people with nature on 127 acres of forest, wetland, and river habitat.

Chattahoochee Riverkeeper (www.chattahoochee.org) works to ensure there is enough clean water in the Chattahoochee River now and for future generations through education, investigations, and advocacy.

EcoAddendum (www.ecoaddendum.org) works to raise awareness about Georgia's rich natural environment and reconnect people with the natural world.

Elachee Nature Science Center (www.elachee.org) promotes environmental understanding through education and conservation.

Flint Riverkeeper (www.flintriverkeeper.org) works to restore and preserve the habitat, water quality, and flow of the Flint River for the benefit of current and future generations and dependent wildlife.

Georgia Conservancy (www.georgiaconservancy.org) protects Georgia through ecological and economic solutions.

Georgia Interfaith Power and Light (www.gipl.org) engages communities of faith in stewardship of creation as a direct expression of faithfulness, serving as a religious response to climate change, environmental injustice, and pollution.

Georgia River Network (www.garivers.org) serves as the voice of Georgia's rivers, working to empower everyone to enjoy, connect with, and advocate for vital and clean flowing rivers.

Georgia Water Coalition (www.gawater.org) is an alliance of more than 250 organizations committed to ensuring that water is managed fairly for all Georgians and protected for future generations.

The Nature Conservancy of Georgia (www.nature.org/en-us) works to create a world where people and nature thrive.

Park Pride (www.parkpride.org) works with communities in the city of Atlanta and DeKalb County to improve their parks.

Partnership for Southern Equity (www.psequity.org) advances policies and institutional actions that promote racial equity and shared prosperity for all in the growth of metro Atlanta and the American South.

Soque River Watershed Association (www.soque.org) works to protect and restore the Soque River, a major tributary to the Chattahoochee River.

Southern Environmental Law Center (www.southernenvironment.org) uses the law to defend and protect our air, water, climate, wildlife, lands, and people.

SouthWings (www.southwings.org) and its volunteer pilots provide partners with a unique aerial perspective to better understand and solve pressing environmental issues in the Southeast.

Upper Chattahoochee Chapter Trout Unlimited (www.ucctu.org) works to protect and restore Georgia's trout coldwater fisheries and their watersheds.

West Atlanta Watershed Alliance (www.wawa-online.org) works to improve the quality of life within the West Atlanta Watershed by protecting, preserving, and restoring our community's natural resources.

National Organizations

American Rivers (www.americanrivers.org) works to protect wild rivers, restore damaged rivers, and conserve clean water for people and nature.

The Conservation Fund (www.conservationfund.org) protects America's legacy of land and water resources through land acquisition and sustainable community and economic development.

National Parks Conservation Association (www.npca.org) is the voice of America's national parks, working to protect and preserve our nation's most iconic and inspirational places.

River Network (www.rivernetwork.org) empowers and unites people and communities to protect and restore rivers and other waters that sustain all life by offering some of the best resources available for people seeking ways to safeguard the waterways. Its resource library (https://www.rivernetwork.org/connect-learn/resources/) includes such publications as *The Clean Water Act Owner's Manual, Drinking Water Guide: A Resource for Advocates, Waste in Our Waters: A Community Toolkit for Aquatic Litter Removal,* and *Tools for Equitable Climate Resilience: Fostering Community-Led Research and Knowledge.*

Sierra Club (www.sierraclub.org), the most enduring and influential grassroots environmental organization in the United States, works to amplify the power of millions of members and supporters to defend everyone's right to a healthy world.

Trust for Public Land (www.tpl.org) creates parks and protects land for people, ensuring healthy, livable communities for generations to come.

Waterkeeper Alliance (www.waterkeeper.org) ensures that the world's Waterkeeper groups are as connected to each other as they are to their local waters, organizing the fight for clean water into a coordinated global movement.

REFERENCES

American Rivers. "Money Pit: The High Cost and High Risk of Water Supply Reservoirs in the Southeast." Apalachicola-Chattahoochee-Flint Stakeholders, July 2012. https://www.acfstakeholders.org/.

Barnes, Roy. "Nature Needs a Voice—for Georgia's Sake." *Atlanta Journal-Constitution*, May 8, 2007.

Berinato, Scott, with David Kessler. "That Discomfort You're Feeling Is Grief." *Harvard Business Review*, March 23, 2020.

Berry, Wendell. "The Peace of Wild Things." In *Openings*, by Wendell Berry. New York: Harcourt, Brace & World, 1968.

Bethea, Charles. "The Mystery of the Headless Goats in the Chattahoochee." *New Yorker*, September 29, 2022.

Blackmon, Douglas. *Slavery by Another Name: The Re-enslavement of Black Americans from the Civil War to World War II.* New York: Anchor, 2008.

Brooks, Paul. *The House of Life: Rachel Carson at Work.* Boston: Houghton Mifflin, 1972.

Brown, Fred, and Sherri M. L. Smith. *The Riverkeeper's Guide to the Chattahoochee.* Atlanta: CI Publishing, 1997.

Burns, Ken, and Duncan Dayton. *The National Parks: America's Best Idea.* New York: Knopf, 2009.

Chattahoochee Riverkeeper. "Filling the Water Gap" Reports, 2011, 2012, and 2019.

Chattahoochee Riverkeeper. "RiverChat" newsletters, 1994–2014.

Chattahoochee RiverLands. https://www.chattahoocheeriverlands.com.

Chattahoochee River National Recreation Area. https://www.nps.gov/chat/index.htm.

Carson, Rachel. *The Edge of the Sea.* Boston: Houghton Mifflin, 1955.

Carson, Rachel. *Silent Spring.* Boston: Houghton Mifflin, 1962.

Charles S. Mott Foundation. Report: "Two Decades of Grantmaking Improved Rivers." July 10, 2019. https://www.mott.org/news/articles/reporting-results-two- decades-of-grantmaking-improved-rivers-strengthened -environmental-groups-in-the-southeastern-u-s/.

Coelho, Paul. *The Pilgrimage.* 1987. New York: HarperCollins, 2008.

Cook, Joe. *Chattahoochee River User's Guide.* Athens: University of Georgia Press, 2014.

Cook, Joe, and Monica Cook. *River Song: A Journey down the Chattahoochee and Apalachicola Rivers.* Tuscaloosa: University of Alabama Press, 2000.

Crawford, Tom. "The Makeup of the DNR Board Is Completed." *Georgia Report,* January 27, 2012.

CRK-TV. "Twenty Years of Progress: Chattahoochee Riverkeeper 20th Anniversary." Vimeo, 2014. https://vimeo.com/130144419.

DeMeo, Terry A., Don R. Christy, and James E. Kundell. "Georgia's Trout Stream Buffer Program Assessment." Carl Vinson Institute of Government, University of Georgia, 2005.

Eiseley, Loren. "The Flow of the River." In *The Immense Journey*. New York: Random House, 1957.

Ferris, Jabr. "The Social Life of Forests." *New York Times*, December 4, 2020.

Franklin, Shirley. "Press Conference Remarks by Shirley Franklin." October 16, 2002.

Georgia Environmental Protection Division. "Fish Consumption Guidelines." 2021. https://epd.georgia.gov/watershed-protection-branch/watershed -planning-and-monitoring-program/fish-consumption-guidelines.

Georgia River Network. "Upper Chattahoochee River Water Trail." https:// garivers.org/water-trails-and-paddling/upper-chattahoochee-river-water-trail/.

Gore, Pamela J. W., and William Witherspoon. *Roadside Geology of Georgia*. Missoula: Mountain Press, 2013.

Grahame, Kenneth. *The Wind in the Willows*. London: Methuen, 1908.

Hamilton, Rich. "How Mushrooms and the Mycelium Network are Healing the World." *Garden Culture*, June 15, 2020.

Hanson, David, and Michael Hanson. "The Last Oyster Tongers of Apalachicola." *The Bitter Southerner,* February 1, 2022.

Haskell, David George. "Beech." *David George Haskell* (blog), December 30, 2012. https://dghaskell.com/2012/12/30/beech/.

Haskell, David George. *The Forest Unseen: A Year's Watch in Nature.* New York: Viking, 2012.

Helton, Charmagne. "Dear EPA: McKinney, Gingrich Agree." *Atlanta Journal-Constitution*, March 27, 1997.

HJacobs Creative. "Neighborhood Water Watch." Vimeo. https://vimeo .com/274865134.

Jehl, Douglas. "Atlanta's Growing Thirst Creates Water War." *New York Times*, May 27, 2002.

Johnson, Terry. "Out My Backdoor: Periodical Cicadas Make Loud Entrance." Wildlife Resources Division, Georgia Department of Natural Resources, May 2011.

Joyner, Chris. "After $16 million, Glades Reservoir Not 'Viable,' State Says." *Atlanta Journal-Constitution*, February 12, 2016.

Joyner, Chris. "Millions in Tax Dollars Wasted on Risky Reservoirs." *Atlanta Journal-Constitution*, December 8, 2016.

Joyner, Chris. "Revolving Door Power Politics." *Atlanta Journal-Constitution*, March 18, 2012.

Kiers, Toby, and Merlin Sheldrake. "A Powerful and Underappreciated Ally in the Climate Crisis? Fungi." *The Guardian*, November 30, 2021.

Kimmerer, Robin Wall. *Braiding Sweetgrass: Indigenous Wisdom, Scientific Knowledge, and the Teachings of Plants*. Minneapolis: Milkweed, 2013.

Kimmerer, Robin Wall. *Gathering Moss: A Natural and Cultural History of Mosses*. Corvallis: Oregon State University Press, 2003.

Krakow, Kenneth K. *Georgia Place-Names*. 3rd ed. Macon: Winship Press, 1994.

Leopold, Aldo. *A Sand County Almanac*. Oxford: Oxford University Press, 1949.

Loeffler, G., J. L. Meyer, H. Trammell, and S. Holmbeck-Pelham. "Fish Consumption Patterns along the Upper Chattahoochee River." Water Resources Conference Proceedings, University of Georgia, April 2003. https://smartech.gatech.edu/bitstream/handle/1853/48346/Loeffler_5.3.2.pdf.

Markham, Beryl. *West with the Night*. 1942. Albany: North Point Press, 1983.

Meyer, Judy L., Krista L. Jones, Geoffrey C. Poole, C. Rhett Jackson, James E. Kundell, B. Lane Rivenbark, Elizabeth L. Kramer, and William Bumback. "Implications of Changes in Riparian Buffer Protection for Georgia's Trout Streams." Institute of Ecology, University of Georgia, 2005.

Oliver, Mary. *Upstream*. London: Penguin, 2016.

Oliver, Mary. "Wild Geese." In *Dream Work*. New York: Atlantic Monthly, 1986.

Rankin, Bill. "Decades before Water Wars, Buford Dam Won City Support, Not Finances." *Atlanta Journal-Constitution*, August 10, 2012.

Sanders, W. Marshall. "Policy and Protest: An Analysis of City Wastewater Treatment Issues." Research Atlanta, 1995.

Saulitis, Eva. *Becoming Earth*. Pasadena: Boreal, 2016.

Seabrook, Charles. "'Death by Pollution': Atlanta's Waste Choking the Life Out of West Point Lake." *Atlanta Journal-Constitution*, October 23, 1988.

Seabrook, Charles. "Return of a River." *Atlanta Journal-Constitution*, January 3, 1999.

Schlanger, Zoe. "Our Silent Partners." *New York Review*, October 7, 2021.

Sheldrake, Melvin. *Entangled Life: How Fungi Make Our Worlds, Change Our Minds, and Shape Our Future*. New York: Random House, 2020.

Shelton, Stacy. "Obituary: Ogden Doremus." *Atlanta Journal-Constitution*, April 6, 2007.

Shepherd, Nan. *The Living Mountain*. Aberdeen: Aberdeen University Press, 1977.

Simard, Suzanne. *Finding the Mother Tree: Discovering the Wisdom of the Forest*. New York: Knopf, 2021.

Snyder, Michael. "Why Do Some Leaves Persist on Beech and Oak Trees Well into Winter?" *Northern Woodlands*, November 22, 2010.

Stone, Emily. "The Wood Wide Web." *Northern Wilds,* October 2017.

Tallamy, Douglas. *The Nature of Oaks: The Rich Ecology of Our Most Essential Native Trees*. New York: Workman, 2021.

Tippett, Krista, with Bryan Stevenson. "Love Is the Motive." *On Being with Krista Tippett*, December 3, 2020.

U.S. Geological Survey. BacteriALERT Monitoring Program. https://www2.usgs .gov/water/southatlantic/ga/bacteria/

U.S. National Park Service. "Chattahoochee River National Recreation Area: Comprehensive Trails Management Plan/Environmental Assessment." 2022.

Visser, Steve. "Huge East Point Oaks a Tough Fight for Preservationists." *Atlanta Journal-Constitution*, December 23, 2011.

Wall, Michael. "Being Harold Reheis." *Creative Loafing*, July 17, 2003.

Wall, Michael. "$1.9 Billion Worth of Tunnel Vision." *Creative Loafing*, April 18, 2001.

Wohlleben, Peter. *The Hidden Life of Trees: What They Feel, How They Communicate*. Vancouver: Greystone, 2015.

World Bank. "High and Dry: Climate Change, Water, and the Economy." 2016.

Wu, Katherine. "Some Trees May 'Social Distance' to Avoid Disease." *National Geographic*, July 6, 2020.